The Nonprofit Organization's Guide to E-Commerce

The Nonprofit Organization's Guide to E-Commerce

Gary M. Grobman

White Hat Communications
Harrisburg, Pennsylvania

The author gratefully acknowledges the contributions made to this book by Gary
B. Grant, the co-author of *The Nonprofit Internet Handbook*. Some of the material
that appears in this book in Appendix A, Appendix B, and Appendix D originally
appeared in that publication, and has been updated.

Printed in the United States of America.
Editing: Linda Grobman, John Hope
Proofreading: Barbara Blank

Library of Congress Card Number: 00-106552

ISBN: 1-929109-03-2

The Nonprofit Organization's Guide to E-Commerce

Table of Contents

What is E-Commerce?
What is the Connection to Nonprofits?
Why Nonprofits Lag Behind Their For-Profit Counterparts
Advantages of E-Commerce Over Traditional Commerce
Build, Buy or Rent
Payment Service Providers
Costs

Introduction
Accepting Payment Over the Internet
E-cash and E-checks
Customer Service
Order Fulfillment
Refund and Returns Policy
Receipts and Invoices
Collecting Taxes
Shipping and Handling
Out-of-Country Sales

Introduction
SSL and Other Encryption Technology
Certification/Authentication
Digital Signatures
Protection of Customer Data
Firewalls
Privacy Policies
Cookies
Copyrights
Trademarks
Unrelated Business Income Taxes (UBIT)

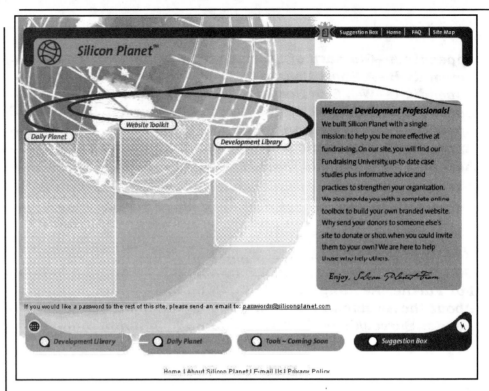

The Silicon Planet home page at: http://www.siliconplanet.com. ©2000. Reprinted with permission.

PART 1
Nonprofits
and
E-Commerce

Introduction

The purpose of this book is to explore how nonprofit organizations can use the power of the Internet to generate more revenues for their organizations. In addition to providing real examples of how organizations are taking advantage of what the Internet has to offer, it offers practical advice on avoiding some of the common mistakes made by those who run nonprofit organizations. It also suggests strategies to build a relationship to potential "customers" who will assist your organization in achieving its vital mission by making donations, participating in advocacy efforts, and creating a community of individuals who are committed to helping the organization achieve its mission and vision.

Innovative communications technologies are revolutionizing the way the world does business. Many feel that we are on the dawn of a second Industrial Revolution. Phrases such as the "New Economy" and "Old Economy" are becoming clichés.

Traditional "old economy" businesses are adopting cutting-edge management practices and new technology. The ubiquitous Nortel Networks (http://www.nortelnetworks.com) commercial that asks, "What do you want the Internet to be?" is increasingly being answered, "Whatever you want it to be!" by thousands of entrepreneurs, backed by venture capitalists, who risk millions of dollars to fill a real or imaginary need. Many who are affiliated with nonprofits want the Internet to help fulfill their social missions, be it advocacy, the delivery of social services, public education, or improving society in a myriad of ways.

One version of that Nortel commercial shows a man and a bovine sitting on the couch. "I want the Internet to be a cash cow," says the man. It is a vision shared by thousands who are investing their life savings in starting "dot-com" companies.

The for-profit world has embraced e-commerce, recognizing that it is the future of how business-to-business (B2B) and business-to-consumer (B2C) purchasing will be conducted by millions, if not billions, of participants. According to a June 2000 analysis by IDC Research, revenues from e-commerce will grow to $1.6 trillion by 2003. According to this study, almost 30% of Internet users will purchase goods or services online by the end of 2000, and 38 percent will have done so by 2003. The average spending per transaction will also increase.

There has also been a staggering increase in the number of new e-commerce-related employment. A Cisco Systems-funded study carried out by the Austin's Center for Research in Electronic Commerce, at the University of Texas, found that 650,000 new jobs were created in 1999 as a result of the Internet economy, bringing the total number of workers to 2.5 million, a 36% increase over 1998. Revenue generated from the Internet increased by 62 percent and totaled $524 billion in 1999.

According to a May 2000 report by Jupiter Communications (http://www.jup.com), Web-impacted spending, which includes both online purchases and Web–influenced off-line purchases, will exceed $235 billion in 2000 and reach more than $831 billion in 2005. Online users in the United States will account for 75 percent of all expected U.S. retail spending (both online and off-line) in 2005, up from 43 percent in 1999. The study didn't look at how much of this retail traffic is accounted for by the nonprofit sector, but all indications are that nonprofit organizations are building and expanding their Web sites to take advantage of this trend.

The business models and strategies used by for-profits can be adapted by nonprofits to generate revenue that will finance the expansion of nonprofit organization programs and activities. At the very least, these new techniques make it a bit easier to raise the funds and thus reduce what must be one of the leading causes of stress and burnout among nonprofit executives and staff—the constant battle to raise dollars to balance organizational budgets.

Technology is Facilitating Changes in Management Structure

Concurrent with the development of new business models, new organizational management models are evolving. This trend is accelerated in part by new communications technology. Boundaries of organizations are blurring. The use of outsourcing, temporary hires, subcontracting, reliance on independent consultants, telecommuting, and cooperative venturing have tested the conventional structure of organizations. Competition and financial stress are motivating mergers, partnerships, collaborations, and joint venturing. It is not unusual for some of these relationships to involve organizations from different sectors.

Even within bounded organizations, hierarchical organizational structures are giving way to team-based entities. Matrix management structures may mean that your supervisor on today's project may be taking direction from you on another project. Networks in which workers employed by a large organization, independent consultants and employees of suppliers (or even direct competitors) coordinate on an ad hoc basis for a common goal, using the Internet to communicate. The "virtual organization" is becoming increasingly common.

Boundaries of entire sectors are blurring as well. A project may find representatives of government, the for-profit sector, and the nonprofit sector sitting around a table (or as is becoming increasingly more common, sitting in front of their computer monitors or participating in a teleconference), sharing information and making decisions. The players may change as the project changes. Depending on the project, a participant may be acting as an agent of the public (government) one day, as a for-profit entrepreneur another day, and as a nonprofit actor a third day.

These changes in management structure are facilitated by advances in information technology. E-commerce can take advantage of the cooperation of people who have loyalties to one organization, several organizations, or no organization. This presents challenges to those who are trying to coordinate the efforts of organizations without clear-cut boundaries. But the advantages of having so many people being able to contribute to a single project perhaps outweighs the disadvantages. What we do know is that there are few nonprofit organizations that engage in an e-commerce effort as Lone Rangers, handling everything in-house. As will be explained, there is really no particular benefit to trying to do all of the work yourself and reinvent the wheel.

Archimedes once said, "Give me a lever long enough and a place to stand, and I will move the world." With today's technology, you can very well say, "Give me a computer, a server, and a good product or service to sell, and I will sell it to the world!"

How To Use This Guide

This guide is designed as a primer for nonprofit executives and staff who want to be a part of the e-commerce revolution. In this book, I share the experiences of nonprofit staff like yourself, many who did not have any particular technology background but recognized the potential of the Internet to increase organizational revenue. I also share the experience of for-profit executives and private consultants who work with nonprofits to maximize the benefit of organizational forays into e-commerce.

I recommend using this guide to—

1. Determine if launching an e-commerce program is right for your organization.

2. Learn about some of the cutting-edge business models that nonprofit organizations are utilizing.

3. Gauge the costs and benefits of each of the options you have, such as buying a custom-designed Web site, developing your Web site in-house, or "renting" a site from a provider.

4. Identify which sites on the Internet have free or low-cost tools for facilitating your e-commerce program.

5. View some of the most successful and eye-pleasing nonprofit e-commerce sites.

6. Learn why writing for the Web is different from writing for conventional media.

7. Find information on important e-commerce issues, such as privacy, security, and copyright.

8. Explore the advantages of creating an online community, with career information, message boards, chat, and, of course, commercial opportunities for your organization.

9. Learn what works in nonprofit e-commerce and what doesn't—from the experiences of experts in the field who are featured in the "Up Close" sidebars at the end of each chapter.

Acknowledgments

Linda Grobman, editor and publisher of *The New Social Worker,* was the principal editor of this book, and worked diligently to make it the best book it could be. She has been an e-commerce pioneer, adding innovations to her own Web site (http://www.socialworker.com) that have been described elsewhere in this book. Gary Grant and I are co-authors of the 1998 book, *The Nonprofit Internet Handbook.* Some of the material in this book was first published in the Handbook, and was updated. I appreciate Gary's willingness to share some of this material. A tip of the hat goes to Dr. John McNutt of Boston University's Department of Social Work, who read the manuscript and made useful comments that were incorporated into this book. I appreciate the willingness of some very busy people to be interviewed for the *Up Close* sidebars and for other parts of this book. Thanks go to the many dot-com companies who granted me permission to use screen shots to illustrate some of the Web sites reviewed in this book.

John Hope edited an early draft of this book, and provided wonderful feedback on how it should be structured, advice I took. Barbara Trainin Blank did her usual professional job of proofreading. Thanks go to Jerry Cianciolo of *Contributions Magazine,* the publication in which earlier versions of some of these chapters first appeared. I received a lot of feedback from these articles as a result of posting them in the Gilbert Center's Online Fundraising mailing list to respond to questions, and I was delighted to hear from practitioners in both the nonprofit community and vendors who serve them about new products and services. Many of their insights found their way into this book.

Nonprofits and E-Commerce

What is E-Commerce?

The term *e-commerce* refers to business that is conducted electronically. It includes the marketing of goods and services, using the Internet to join an organization or subscribe to a publication or mailing list, and automated customer service. Technically, using the telephone to place an order qualifies as e-commerce. So would using your debit card to make a purchase at your local convenience store. This book uses a more narrow definition, becoming increasingly common in books and articles to describe business conducted over the Internet. This book will focus on how nonprofit organizations can use the Internet to generate donations, increase membership, market products and services, and respond to customer inquiries and complaints.

What is the Connection to Nonprofits?

Customer service? Marketing? Products? Why do any of this have anything to do with the nonprofit sector?

Many of us lose sight of the fact that a nonprofit organization is a form of business. There are distinctions between nonprofits and for-profits. Among them are the principle purpose (i.e., accomplishing a particular mission, compared to making money), governance structure (members of the community with diverse backgrounds compared to businessmen and women), the level of public accountability (substantial compared to minimal), and destination of net revenue (required to further the purposes of a nonprofit organization rather than go into the pockets of the owners). Charities benefit from donations made to them by businesses and individuals who support their mission and purposes. The nonprofit sector also relies on the generous support of the half of American adults who volunteer on behalf of nonprofits, generating the equivalent of more than $200 billion annually in free labor.

Yet nonprofits and for-profits have many things in common. Both need capital to launch their operations, both need cash flow to pay their bills in a timely manner, and both need revenues to pay for staff, supplies, utilities, rent, equipment, printing, and other goods and services. Charities typically receive revenues beyond what is gratuitously donated by the public, the business community, or foundations. For example, they sell services. It is typical that a third or more of the revenue from a social service agency comes from user fees. While many agencies charge on a sliding scale based on income, it is not unusual for them to charge a market rate to those who can afford to pay and use the surplus so generated to cross-subsidize those who cannot afford to pay the full costs of services. Many for-profit firms engage in this strategy as well.

During the recession of the 1980s, many charities were hit by the double whammy of decreased government support coupled with declining donations from the public. Entrepreneurial nonprofit organizations began to devise innovative solutions to revenue shortfalls. Use of the World Wide Web was a natural extension of time-honored strategies for increasing organizational revenues, such as soliciting for organizational memberships, conducting auctions, selling fundraising event tickets, retailing standard "gift shop" items, and hawking organizational publications. The Internet provided a new medium for innovative strategies to increase revenue.

Why Nonprofits Lag Behind Their For-Profit Counterparts

It is no secret that organizations in the voluntary sector lag behind their for-profit counterparts when it comes to innovation. "Nonprofit organizations have been slow to adopt technology," writes Boston College's Dr. John McNutt, one of the few academics publishing empirical articles about how nonprofits are using the Internet. "While e-mail has become a widespread practice that is comprehended by many nonprofit practitioners, many of the other technologies are not so well understood."

Dr. McNutt's 1999 study of how United Ways are using the Internet for fundraising points to the fact that traditional workplace giving methodology needs to change because the nature of the workplace is changing. There is more telecommuting, and a growing "contingent" workforce that does not have the same organizational loyalty. "This makes the traditional campaign strategies more expensive and reduces the economies of scale present in current campaigns," McNutt observes. He sees technological innovation as a way to respond to these developments.

Many more organizations are fundraising in the workplace in direct competition with United Ways, and competition for philanthropic support is increasingly keen. Technology is fueling some of this competition. United Way organizations, through their contacts with the business community, are well-positioned to lead the nonprofit sector into the Information Age, McNutt suggests.

I used to joke that to many charity executives, upgrading technology involved trading in their trusty manual Remington typewriters for IBM Selectrics. While those days are long gone, it is not unusual for nonprofit organizations to be brought into the computer age solely because of a for-profit that generously donated a nearly-obsolete computer. Frankly, that was how the nonprofit organization I ran got its first PC. It took several weeks of not being able to get it to do a thing before someone pointed out that this particular computer had a network card in it, making it useless as a stand-alone computer. Once that barrier was overcome, this computer became a powerful, time-saving tool—at least when I was able to make it function as I intended.

That was more than 15 years ago. Today, some of the computers that get dropped off at the doorsteps of charities like unwanted infants have more computer power than the systems that the Apollo astronauts used to navigate to the moon. While 21st century charities are more sophisticated than their ancestors, there may always be a gap between the capabilities of the for-profit and nonprofit sectors.

One obvious factor for this disparity is money. It is part of the capitalist mindset that it takes an investment to make money. Whether it is building a Web site, investing in computer servers, buying the best available software, or hiring an experienced Webmaster to create a site that encourages repeat visitors, the for-profit community seems to have grasped the potential of e-commerce far better than the nonprofit sector.

Nonprofit organizations are adapting new business models for fundraising, friendraising, and partnering. Innovative business models are continuing to evolve. Many of these have applications to generating revenue for charities and other nonprofits.

It is difficult to find nonprofits that do not routinely engage in a substantial number of business transactions of one kind or another. Even the few that donate all of their services to the needy and are run strictly by volunteers still purchase equipment, pay for postage and envelopes, and print brochures to publicize their cause. Most nonprofits charge something for their services, often on a sliding scale based upon income. The difference between costs and charges is made up from donations from the public, grants from public and private foundations, government subsidies of one form or another, and miscellaneous income. For years, charities have generated such income through a variety of programs and activities, such as selling newsletter subscriptions and other publications, collecting fees at conferences and workshops, operating thrift shops, conducting flea markets and running races, renting mailing lists, conducting auctions, scheduling fundraising dinners, and selling group outings to sports events or theater performances.

The World Wide Web has made all of this easier, at least for many organizations, in two significant ways. First, it has provided organizations with a way to reach almost everyone, and to do this quickly and inexpensively. Using a combination of strategies, such as conventional mail, telephone, and media advertising, along with Web postings, mailing list postings, broadcast e-mail, and Web advertising, an organization can reach its target market and expand its reach beyond that. Second, using sophisticated technology, organizations can take advantage of homebound volunteers (at one end of the scale) and pricey, professional "back-end" providers (at the other end of the scale) to do much of the work.

New business models have emerged that permit nonprofit organizations to take advantage of technology and raise funds that would not have come their way otherwise. One obvious example is the "affiliate" model pioneered by Amazon.com. That Seattle-based company simply announced to the world that by linking to its Web site, purchases of books, CDs, DVDs, videos, electronics, software, video games, toys, or home improvement items that are generated by that link will earn a commission.

The only qualification for joining this program is to have a Web site. Joining involves visiting the Amazon.com site, clicking on the "Join Associates" link at the bottom of the home page, electronically submitting a form provided on the site (after reading and agreeing to the operating agreement), and using tools provided on the site to set up your preferred way to link to Amazon.com and promote the collaboration.

To date, more than 400,000 individuals and organizations have become Amazon.com associates, including some of the company's competitors, such as Yahoo! and America Online. For nonprofits and for-profits alike, this simple, yet revolutionary, business model is generating valuable revenue without the need for any additional investment or exposure to risk.

Other new business models are also taking hold. Chapter 6 and Chapter 7 are devoted to two of these— the online shopping mall and online auction. Most of us are already familiar with what is being called "dynamic pricing" models. Online auctions are an example of one such dynamic pricing model, which is effective when the supply of a good is low, and the demand is high. I've participated in another dynamic pricing model, used by priceline.com, in which the supply of a good (in my case, an airline seat that would otherwise be unfilled) is high and the demand is low. No doubt, these business models have been around for many years, even before anyone ever heard of a computer. But the problem was that it was resource-consuming to make the match between buyers and sellers, and then negotiate an agreement. With the new technology, bringing the buyer and seller together and reaching an agreement on price can be achieved almost instantaneously, and for almost no cost. This is powerful, and is changing the way our entire economy operates.

Surely, other models will develop. As I write, new entrants into the market, each with their individualized spin on a business model, are publicizing their launches, many backed by tens of millions of dollars. A "Click to Give" site such as Charity Frogs (http://www.charityfrogs.com) pledges to donate $1 to the American Red Cross, up to $1 million, for each unique computer whose user clicks on the site, once per day. As I write this, more than a half million dollars have been pledged. When I clicked, I got a message thanking me, and a link to a commercial shoe company that sponsored the site.

What does the Red Cross, one of the largest charities in the world with a $2.3 billion annual budget, think of this?

"We are thrilled to have Internet entrepreneurs contributing to our organization in such a significant way," said Jennifer Dunlap, senior vice president at the American Red Cross in a December 1999 press release announcing the partnership. "In addition to their financial contribution, (Charity Frogs) is also helping to raise awareness of the work of the American Red Cross in the Internet community. The American Red Cross is always looking for creative methods to reach more people, and this innovative effort has the potential to make a tremendous impact in the lives of the families we help each year."

"We believe that helping out charitable organizations such as the American Red Cross is very important," said Tony Hsieh, one of the entrepreneurs who devised the Charity Frogs concept. "But at the same time, we wanted to do something fun, interesting, and reflective of our Internet backgrounds."

Visit The Hunger Site (http://www.thehungersite.com) and click on the "Donate Free Food" icon that results in the site sponsors making a donation to a food bank. Each sponsor pays one-half cent per donation, which buys a quarter cup of food. When I clicked last, there were six sponsors. According to information on the site, more than 200 metric tons of food had been donated weekly to the United Nations World Food Programme. Click on the "shopping" icon and you are transported to an online shopping mall, where up to 15% of the purchase price is donated to the UN food program.

You can find other beneficiaries of related sites at: http://clickandsave.8k.com.

Netcentives is the parent company of ClickRewards and manages ClickRewards' nonprofit promotions, Click2Give (http://www.netcentives.com or http://www.clickrewards.com). ClickRewards provides incentives to members to donate to various charities, such as rewarding them with ClickMiles, frequent flyer miles on ten major airlines that can also be redeemed for merchandise and hotel stays.

"ClickMiles have proven to be a powerful incentive," reports Meg Garlinghouse, who manages the cause-related marketing division for the San Francisco-based marketing company Netcentives. "We have had terrific results with our nonprofit partners to date. Last year, World Wildlife Fund increased their online donations by 235% the month that we ran the promotion, and increased their average donation by 24%." Among other participating charities are the Special Olympics, CARE, Rainforest Action Network, and Toys for Tots.

"The best part of the Netcentives' Click2Give program is the low cost to the nonprofit," Garlinghouse says. "We provide our nonprofit partners with free e-mail marketing. We have the potential to reach millions and we believe that we can make a difference by using this technology to connect people to the important causes they care about. For these reasons, more and more nonprofits are using this as a fundraising strategy."

In April 2000, the firm's "Miles for the Wild" campaign raised over $400,000 in just five weeks for the World Wildlife Fund.

Few of the commercial sites that specifically target themselves to the needs of the nonprofit community make a profit. Perhaps few will *ever* make a profit. It is too early to forecast where all of this is heading, but the entrepreneurial spirit of our American culture remains impressively robust (even in the face of some recent spectacular dot-com failures). Our cousins to the North and South are catching up to us with respect to Internet access, and Europe is not far behind; in fact many of the most creative e-commerce applications are coming from Sweden, Israel, and Great Britain, and are finding their way to the New Land.

Advantages of E-Commerce Over Traditional Commerce

As a result of e-mail, the World Wide Web, electronic mailing lists, and real time chat, the velocity of business transactions has made a quantum leap. The Internet has salient advantages over conventional methods of sales marketing, such as:

1. *You can harness the World Wide Web to lower overall costs.*

    Imagine how much you save in time and money by writing a short message about your organization's new shopping mall site and sending a broadcast e-mail to everyone on your newsletter mailing list. Brochures do not need to be designed, printed, stuffed into envelopes, and mailed. Once you pay for Internet access, no additional fee is involved in sending these messages over the Internet. Compare the relative costs of having a "virtual" thrift shop and one consisting of bricks and mortar.

2. *You are capable of reaching a global, targeted market virtually instantaneously.*

    Once you have a site up, you are accessible to more than a quarter of a billion people worldwide, with the number expected to reach a half billion by 2003. With the use of search engines, Web rings, electronic mailing lists, online communities, and similar innovations, those with an affinity with your organization have ways to find you, even if you lack the marketing savvy or resources to find them.

3. *Your "store" is open 24 hours/day, seven days/week, and always has free parking.*

    This means more than being accessible to those in faraway time zones. Sometimes, people are more willing to shop when the mood hits them, and that mood may occur at 3 a.m. It is certainly more convenient to make a purchase from one's home compared to visiting a store, and there is immediate satisfaction (make that "immediate gratification") in placing an order from a computer compared to waiting for snail mail to arrive. Innovative software is evolving that seeks to make the online shopping experience comparable to what occurs in a real store, with shoppers being able to chat with each other in real time and exchange comments about their prospective purchases.

4. *You can level the playing field between organizations with many more resources than yours.*

    It takes a lot of resources to build and staff a bricks and mortar store, such as Macy's or the gift shop that is located in the Metropolitan Museum of Art in New York. A pre-teen with a minimum of computer savvy and a Web site host can use free software to create a store that looks sophisticated, and can handle almost all of the financial transactions that are required—although Mom or Dad will still have to sign the agreements to establish a credit card merchant account.

5. *You can consummate business transactions electronically without the need for expensive labor or intermediaries such as brokers.*

   Again, sophisticated software, much of it available free for downloading, handles all of the dirty work involved in making the sale from an online catalog, charging the right shipping and handling, calculating sales tax, sending acknowledgments and receipts, and helping with fulfillment. Intermediaries such as traditional office-based stock brokers, insurance agents, bankers, and travel agents are finding that e-commerce business models are making their jobs anachronisms.

6. *You can harness the strength of search engines and directories to facilitate your potential customers finding you.*

   Research by Integrated Marketing & Technology (http://www.tech-work.com) has shown that by an overwhelming margin, more people find a Web site through a search engine than through any other strategy (see page 100), such as direct advertising, word-of-mouth, or by chance through surfing. By using little tricks (see chapter 9) to insert the right metatags in your file and writing the words to facilitate search engine searches, those who are interested in your site have a good chance of finding you.

7. *You can automate customer service.*

   A simple Frequently Asked Questions (FAQ) file posted on your site is likely to answer more than half of the questions you would otherwise have to answer by telephone or mail using personal staff. Using electronic forms, you can eliminate much of the confusion and delay that occur when customers have to tell and retell their story. Using a form, they write about the problem once, and you can electronically route the communication to the person who can rectify the problem.

8. *You can take advantage of the expertise and labor of literally thousands of organizations that will do the work you need done, and make it appear to your customer that they are all working for your organization.*

   What this means is that you can go back to focusing on your organization's mission rather than worrying about how to design and maintain your Web site and handle electronic fundraising and sales. The virtual, ad hoc organization is becoming institutionalized as a result of e-commerce business models.

Here are some trends that bode well for nonprofit e-commerce:

1. *The "velocity" of communication is increasing exponentially.* One manifestation of this is the degree to which warnings about the "I Love You" virus swept through corporate and personal e-mail sys-

tems in April 2000, unfortunately, too late to avoid serious damage to thousands of systems. The e-mail dissemination of jokes and the stories that create urban legends (http://urbanlegends.com) are other examples of the "contagious" nature of the spread of information over the Internet. People belong to online communities. Posting to one often results in that post being spread to other mailing lists.

One-to-one communication has also accelerated. Written communications used to take several days to be exchanged. Today, that exchange occurs in seconds. Business deals that once took weeks or months are consummated in the blink of an eye. Almost all of the interviews for this book were conducted through e-mail, taking a fraction of the time to complete compared to face-to-face interviews or even telephone interviews.

2. *"Transaction costs" have decreased.* At almost every step in the business process, time has been compressed, and costs have become almost negligible. Creating the product, finding potential customers, luring customers to the "store," providing the information necessary to foster a buying decision, processing the transaction, fulfilling the order, sending an order confirmation, and informing the customers about new products and services can all be accomplished electronically with little or no incremental cost.

3. *The "playing field" has been leveled.* The smallest nonprofit can create a sophisticated Web site with e-commerce functions that has the look and feel of the largest nonprofits with full-time Webmasters. As the caption of the most famous Internet-related *New Yorker* cartoon says, "On the Internet, no one knows you are a dog." The price of entry into building an e-commerce site for the typical nonprofit is a few dollars a month for a host and some sweat equity. There are many Web-hosting services that will provide free Web space for nonprofits, including some of the online shopping mall services described in Chapter 6. This is a two-edged sword. Frauds and scams flourish over the Internet, and information appears that is not credible, simply because someone posted it without checking out the facts.

4. *Information is almost all "free," along with breathtakingly sophisticated software.* Of course, there is content on the Web you can pay for. The Web could have gone a pay-as-you-go route—charging you a nickel for each time you used a search engine, or a dollar for every time you downloaded a software program. Fortunately (at least I think so), the technology for keeping track of small financial transactions did not keep pace with the movement to finance Web sites with advertising. As a result, most of the information you need from the Internet can be found for free. We have become spoiled, and expect to maintain this almost universally free resource. Web sites such as commercial newspapers that sought to charge "subscribers" found extensive resistance. Many that charged for access have recognized that it is futile to try to change the Internet culture that has developed, which insists on free access to information on the Web.

5. *Opportunities for marketing using new business models have sky-rocketed.* As previously mentioned, for-profit companies have developed new business models that permit charities to benefit either directly or indirectly. Some of this is the result of corporate executives having a socially responsible streak, and recognizing that it is everyone's responsibility to respond to societal needs. And some of this is simple business sense, recognizing that it is possible to make a buck by providing services to charities. Regardless of the motivation, the "halo effect" encourages the public to donate to charities (a record $190 billion was donated to charity in 1999 in the United States, according to a survey released May 24, 2000, by Giving USA). And billions of dollars more were generated by charities from commercial ventures which, more and more, are benefiting from the World Wide Web.

6. *People want to choose where their donations go and find out more about their charities.* There are plenty of Internet sites that are willing to provide information useful to donors, such as GuideStar (http://www.guidestar.org), Council of Better Business Bureaus (http://www.bbb.org), and the National Charities Information Bureau (http://www.give.org).

7. *Competition on the World Wide Web has increased.* In February 2000, the number of unique World Wide Web pages surpassed one billion. Hundreds of new dot-com startups have been announced since then, many of which target nonprofits in one way or another. Internet surfers are being pulled in many different directions in many different new ways. Online communities generally increase the visit time of viewers. Animations; free files; contests with million dollar prizes; one-stop communities that offer news, weather, sports, search engines, directories, stock quotes, chat rooms, message boards (and, of course, shopping!) vie with each other for market share. There are hundreds of free sites that appeal to those interested in the nonprofit sector, and all are vying for the same limited audience.

Build, Buy, or Rent

An organization's Web site is the most visible ingredient of a nonprofit organization's e-commerce strategy. You have three basic choices in deciding which direction to go, and making the choice depends on factors such as—

- the amount of financial investment you are prepared to make;
- the amount of staff time you are willing to devote to building, maintaining, and troubleshooting;
- whether you are comfortable with "off the rack" features or want a site that is state-of-the-art and custom-made;
- your comfort level with outside vendors having access to your financial transactions;
- whether you want to have complete control over your Web site so that, for example, you don't have to depend on private companies to update files when they have the time;
- whether you are comfortable with paying an outside firm based on the amount of the fundraising that is transacted on the site; and
- the importance to you of having all visitors stay on your site rather

than being routed to a private vendor who may subject the visitor to advertising that your organization cannot control, or which may be inconsistent with your organization's values.

Build: Almost all of the tools a nonprofit needs to build a credible e-commerce site can be found using the links at http://www.onlineorders.net. Here you can find shopping carts, security software, domain name services, bank card services, associate programs, auction software, and Web site promotional services. Much of the software can be downloaded for free.

If you decided you wanted to purchase *The Nonprofit Organization's Guide to E-Commerce* online, you would go to the White Hat Communications Web site (http://www.socialworker.com) and look for the section on the site where books are sold, or the company's nonprofit page (http://www.socialworker.com/nonprofit/nphome.htm). When you click to order this book, you are taken to White Hat's online store hosted free of charge using one of the resources listed at http://www.onlineorders.net.

Other bells and whistles on the home page of this site were free, such as a "refer this page to a friend" form, a language translation service, chat room, message board, and Web statistics program. This entire site was designed and built by my wife, Linda Grobman, the president and founder of White Hat Communications, who is a social worker with no formal IT training.

For those large organizations that have resources to have in-house Webmasters such as the American Red Cross (http://www.redcross.org) and the American Lung Association (http://www.lungusa.org), creating the Web site infrastructure to accept donations online using a secure form was one of their first priorities.

Buy: If you are as well-heeled as the Metropolitan Museum of Art (http://www.metmuseum.org), you can afford to buy the very best. From the looks of this site, it would not be unreasonable to expect this organization's investment in hiring a private firm to custom-design a Web site will result in financial dividends over the long run.

Everything about this site is, pardon the pun, state of the art.

The Metropolitan Museum of Art in New York was visited by 5.2 million people in 1999. Impressive. Yet this number is likely dwarfed by the number of Web surfers from all over the world who visited the museum's Web site at without leaving their computer room. More than 3,000 pieces from the museum's collection are on display at the Web site, along with information about events, programs for kids, and information about a generous percentage of the 2.2 million works in the collection. As an art museum, the Metropolitan Museum hosts many masterpieces. As an example of what one can do with Internet technology, this Web site is a masterpiece itself.

The commercial areas of this site are tasteful, and do not detract from the educational value of the site and the image of the institution, founded in 1870, and housed in an elegant, palatial building located in Central Park.

Viewers looking at a particular piece of art are alerted to related links on the site that provide information about exhibits, and the availability of reproductions for sale. E-commerce opportunities are integrated into the educational content. The store offers books, music, videos, CD-ROMs and other educational materials, as well as jewelry, sculpture, posters, clothing, tableware, perfume, and even Christmas tree ornaments. Members receive a 10% discount, and memberships are available online in more than a dozen categories, each with its benefits succinctly described, and priced ranging from $45 (associate member) to $6,000 (patron, which presumably entitles you to call yourself a patron of the arts). Click on "Support the Met" from the home page, and color-coded pages encourage you to participate in making donations, attending benefits, participate in planned giving, join as a member, and sponsoring specific museum programs. It's easy to contribute online using a secure form (a minimum $25 gift is suggested). Security and privacy statement files are posted. Nearly a dozen files explain what happens to the information when you sign the site guestbook, make a purchase from the store, how site cookies are used, and other transaction information.

This site was custom-designed by a locally based outside firm, Icon Nicholson (http://www.nny.com/nny/). Icon Nicholson is one of many commercial firms that your organization can turn to if you choose to "buy" your Web-based, e-commerce solution.

"This new site is a tremendous asset for both the museum and the art community worldwide," explained Tom Nicholson, co-managing director of Icon Nicholson in a company press release. "It will help attract more visitors to the museum, expand its retail sales through easy-to-use online shopping, and allow those who can't otherwise visit the Met to nonetheless experience its richness over the Internet."

Rent: Application Service Providers, or ASPs (also beginning to refer to their services as online fundraising suites), are sprouting up and are beginning to advertise in the nonprofit national media about the availability of their services. In this context, renting involves purchasing services from a firm of this type who will, for a monthly or annual fee, "rent" you a customized site based on a template. The fundraising pages usually reside on the server of the ASP.

In April 2000, GivingCapital, one such Philadelphia-based startup that raised $2.2 million in 1999 to begin operations, convinced 50 nonprofits to install the company's click-to-give technology on their sites. Among them are the Painted Bride, Brandywine Workshop, and Chester County Historical Society, New York's Do Something Foundation, the Rock and Roll Hall of Fame in Cleveland and the Elizabeth Glaser Pediatric AIDS Foundation in Los Angeles. The program includes the use of an engine technology, for which a patent is pending, that participating charities can use to set up an online matching gift campaign. The software provided is designed to integrate seamlessly into a charity's existing Web site. It also has the capability of offering detailed, real-time analysis of donations made on the site. A service fee is charged by the company based on the amount of donations that are processed through the site.

Other examples of ASPs are LocalVoice (http://www.LocalVoice.com), Entango (http://www.entango.com), and e-Contributor (http://www.econtributor.com).

"In essence, a donation is the end result of a fruitful partnership between an organization and a member," says Robert Kusel, managing director of business development for LocalVoice.com. "The Web offers the potential for achieving just that at a fraction of what it costs these organizations using traditional methods."

Kusel, who previous served as the Director of Major Gifts at Stanford University, and Director of Development and Alumni Affairs at Connecticut's Hotchkiss School, recognizes that the key element of a successful fundraising strategy is to build a strong, long-term relationship between the organization and the donor. "In a nutshell, LocalVoice.com offers organizations a suite of Web-based applications to develop and maintain meaningful relationships with their membership online," he says. "Effective fundraising on the Internet is much more than just offering donation capabilities through a Web site, though that's certainly part of the equation. It's about using the Web to meaningfully engage and communicate with donors on a variety of different levels."

"LocalVoice.com provides a suite of Web-based solutions (accessible from any personal computer, using a username and password) that are self-service solutions for the end clients to utilize as they wish. The applications serve up templates that the client populates and keep the same look-and-feel of their Web sites," he says. Among clients using the service are Ohio Wesleyan University (http://web.owu.edu), St. Mark's School of Texas (http://www.smtexas.org), the San Francisco Food Bank (http://www.sffoodbank.org), the YMCA of San Francisco (http://www.ymcasf.org), and the Contra Costa Humane Society (http://www.cchumane.org).

"We feel strongly that the client organization's Web site will (and in some cases already does) reflect well what it does off-line, and cyberspace provides a real opportunity to engage members online, from all over the United States and beyond," he continues. "Thus our e-mail marketing engine allows organizations to communicate with members for whom they have an accurate e-mail address. The registration and membership functionalities allow efficient e-commerce interaction between the organization and its members, and the donation functionality allows members to show their appreciation for the relationship they have with their organization."

Payment Service Providers

A less sophisticated business model is being touted by vendors who simply offer the service of enabling organizations to accept credit card donations. Fees are either based on the amount of each gift, a flat fee per transaction, or a monthly flat fee. Among the vendors that offer this service are Remit.com (http://www.remit.com) and DonorNet (http://www.donornet.com).

Using Remit.com, individuals may send donations to a charity (or any other business or individual) simply by providing the beneficiary's e-mail address. Charities can accept donations or payments for goods and services without their own merchant accounts. A participating charity can use the firm to collect payments for fundraising events, conventional donations, or the purchase of social services. Included are payment options other than standard credit cards, such as electronic checks and digital currency. Information at this site touts the service as offering "robust fraud protection, industry-leading verification, and reliability."

DonorNet.com, a Colorado-based startup with a division that caters to the needs of nonprofit charities, offers similar services and more. In addition to having the capability to collect and process online donations, the company also offers database administration, pledge and membership enrollment, event registration, ticket sales, auctions and product sales. For umbrella fundraising organizations such as United Ways and Women's Way and corporate employee giving programs, the firm offers Give@Work software, a suite of Web-based tools that automate employee pledge submission and campaign management. According to information from the company's Web site, this software can be customized to meet organizational charitable objectives, provides for various payment options including payroll deduction, and integrates with existing user databases while maintaining an organization's control over donor data to address security and privacy concerns (see: http://donornet.com/giveatwork/index.htm).

Costs

What will all of this cost you? Surprisingly, less than you think in money (but likely more than you think in time). Here are some typical costs.

Web site hosting. Hosting services can be free (see page 166). A typical charge is $10/month.

Domain Name Registration. This costs $35 annually, although there are discounts for pre-payment, and some registrars provide additional discounts.

Search Engine Registration. I recommend you do this by yourself, although you can pay $30-$100 on up for a service to provide this.

Software. Web page construction software such as Microsoft's FrontPage or Adobe PageMill (which is not being sold anymore at Adobe's Web site), which include templates for professionally designed pages, can be purchased for under $100 from discount software companies. Some software can be downloaded from the Internet for free. The latest versions of standard word processing programs are capable of saving files in HTML format. An HTML page can be constructed entirely by using Windows Notepad. Shopping carts can be free (e.g., http://www.freemerchant.com) or cost thousands of dollars. Many accessories that are great on a Web site, such as counters, "send to a friend" forms, and language translators, are available free.

Content. Most nonprofit sites create their own content. It is not unusual to make a purchase or two of graphics or photographs suitable for the Web, but there are many sources that provide these for free.

Site Maintenance. It takes time to update Web sites and respond to feedback from visitors. Some organizations are large enough to hire full-time Webmasters to design and maintain sites, and some have the executive director do this in his or her spare time.

Hardware. If you have a remote virtual Web site host, you don't need anything more than your standard office computer and monitor, which you can buy for perhaps $1,000 for an entire system, including CPU with modem, monitor, and color printer.

Marketing. This can be your largest cost. Advertising the site through print publications, postcards, press releases, banner advertising on other sites, and similar strategies can bring more visitors, but can be expensive.

The bottom line is you can spend as little or as much as you want, but it is possible to obtain everything you need to set up an e-commerce site on your existing Web site at no cost. If you do not yet have a site (or even a computer), you can buy everything you need for a one-time investment of $1,000, and a monthly payment of about $10.

The entire cost can be funded by a donor, or by a businessperson willing to sponsor the site in exchange for placing a banner ad or other acknowledgment on the site's home page.

Up Close:

Dr. John McNutt

Boston College School of

Social Work

Dr. John McNutt is a social work educator who teaches at Boston College. Much of his research focus has been to determine how nonprofit organizations are using technology, and he is collaborating with a colleague, Dr. Steve Hicks, on a book about organizing and advocacy on the Internet. He is also engaged in several research projects on various issues concerning technology and the nonprofit sector. His interest in the nonprofit sector was nurtured by his experiences as a VISTA volunteer in Alabama during the mid 1970s. He went into social work because he says he was interested in making systems work better for the people they serve. His research into nonprofit organizations was an outgrowth of his commitment to social justice.

Dr. McNutt is enthusiastic about sharing why the nonprofit sector should be motivated to take advantage of the economic opportunities provided by the World Wide Web.

"One reason the nonprofit sector should pay attention to e-commerce is competition," he says. "Our traditional turf is sought after by business and government—not to mention other nonprofits. The more critical issue is *service*. As funds get tighter, the difference between adequate service to stakeholders might well be technology. We are also seeing a generation emerge that is comfortable with technology and prefers the convenience that technology can provide."

McNutt points out that nonprofit organizations typically come to the table with a different value base than the for-profit vendors who are trying to convince them to participate in for-profit partnerships. He suggests that both the for-profit vendor and nonprofit client learn to recognize this difference in perspective, and take that into account when they interact. For-profit companies that respect the values of nonprofits will do better in the long run, McNutt predicts.

What are some of the factors that contribute to a successful e-philanthropy effort?

McNutt contends that it is too early to draw any conclusions yet. "Certainly the large national charities, such as the Red Cross, have sophisticated and well executed approaches, and some of the local United Ways seem to be doing a pretty good job," he comments. "The ultimate outcome is how these online strategies support the overall mission and make possible better services.

"We know a lot about the diffusion of technology into organizations," he observes. "Everett Rogers tells us that if technology is reliable, compatible with the organization's system, available on a trial basis, easy to use and better than the alternatives, it will be more likely to be used. We also know that you need good training and technical support."

What advice does he give to the nonprofit executive who is clueless about how the new technology and new business models are providing opportunities for revenue growth, but wants to get started?

"Talk to your fellow executives and knowledgeable people on your board," he recommends. "(Gary) Grobman and (Gary) Grant's *Non-Profit Internet Handbook* is also a great resource for the basics of how to use the Internet for a variety of functions, such as advocacy, building a Web page, and finding resources on the Internet."

Dr. McNutt is ambivalent about whether nonprofits should expect to be able to build and maintain their sites in-house or hire outside professionals. "There is no substitute for having a competent technical support person on staff," he says. "On the other hand, some special skills require consultants. Like everything else, a good plan is needed. After that, you can decide what things are best done internally and what should be outsourced."

Are nonprofit organizations prepared for today's technological opportunities and challenges? "Being 100% prepared today is not enough," he warns. "The younger generation is much more Internet-savvy than other generations and may forgo donations and other involvement, such as volunteering and advocacy, to organizations that don't meet their needs or work the way that they work. Since they've been weaned on computers and the Internet, they may become accustomed to communicating with charities by computer."

Is anything being lost by conducting our "business" over the Internet rather than face-to-face?

"Of course there is—the personal touch, some of the relationship," he points out. "But putting that aside, there are substantial benefits to be gained. Technology is about relationships and personalization—not about computers. Look at how some of the e-commerce sites treat you as an individual. Quite a few nonprofits have a bad record for consumer service. It is easy to be treated impersonally by a real person."

 As an academic researcher, Dr. McNutt is intrigued by all of the venture capital that is pouring into dot-com startup companies that market their services to nonprofit organizations, many of which are in direct competition for the same market. "The simple fact is that most startups are likely to fail and usually for predictable reasons such as poor management, inadequate capitalization, and inadequate marketing," he predicts. "Most of the practitioners that I speak with are fairly sure that competition is as fierce as it's ever been and likely to get even more predatory."

In 1998, McNutt collaborated with Kate Boland and Jennifer Bartron on a research study using content analysis to look at how United Ways utilized their Web sites for fundraising, and reported findings that may have some relevance to the rest of the voluntary sector.

"What we learned is that organizations vary in the ways that they go about using cyberspace as a source of funds," he reports. "Some are interested in the Web as an advertising venue. Others see it as part of the new workplace and aggressively bring their effort to bear on making it a success. Another thing that was obvious to me is that it is critical to update your site on a regular basis and to make the best use of the tools that you have available. I recommend that nonprofit executives take a look at the empirical research being carried out and try to learn from it. There are lots of resources about this research on the web, including the site of the Association for Research on Nonprofit Organizations and Voluntary Action (ARNOVA, http://www.arnova.org). As an academic, I benefit from my contacts in the practice community. I hope that my colleagues who are still practitioners benefit from what my fellow researchers and I have to share."

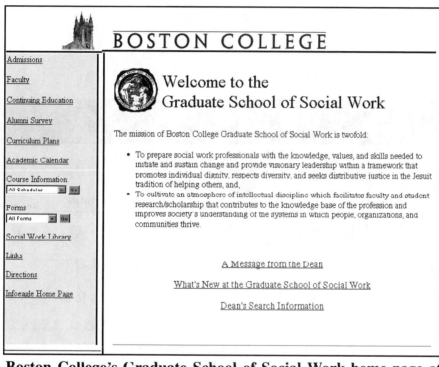

Boston College's Graduate School of Social Work home page at http://www.bc.edu/bc_org/avp/gssw/gssw.htm. Reprinted with permission.

Order ID#100000001152277				
Item	**Qty**	**Price Per Item**	**Total Price**	**Remove?**
The Nonprofit Handbook, 2nd Ed.	1	$ 29.95	$ 29.95	☐
The Nonprofit Internet Handbook	1	$ 29.95	$ 29.95	☐
Improving Quality and Performance in Your Nonprofit Organization	1	$ 16.95	$ 16.95	☐
(If you make changes or check remove, click "update")			$ 76.85	

home ○
view cart ●
company ○
order status ●
privacy policy ○
shipping policy ●

[update]

[continue shopping]

[checkout]

The New Social Worker shopping cart page, accessed at: http://whitehat.safeshopper.com. Reprinted with permission.

Chapter 2

10-Step Quick-Start Guide

In the following chapters, I will provide details on how you can participate in the e-commerce revolution and reap rewards, both financial and other, for your nonprofit organization. The purpose of this chapter is to provide a quick overview of what is involved in setting up an e-commerce site that will sell goods and services for your organization, and a convenient checklist. For perhaps more than 95% of nonprofit organizations, the model I will write about in this chapter will be perfectly sufficient. You will learn about other ways of setting up your site in subsequent chapters. By reviewing this Quick Start Guide, you should get a good idea about what you need to set up an e-commerce operation on your site, and the costs in time and money for doing so. If you've already completed some of these steps, check them off and move down the list.

❒ *Step 1. Choose an ISP (see Appendix C).* Many organizations already have one that provides an online community (such as AOL), e-mail accounts, access to the World Wide Web, and content such as news and weather. Prices are dropping for these services, and many firms now offer them for free.

❒ *Step 2. Choose a Web site host (see Appendix C).* This host can be your ISP or a different provider. Your HTML Web site pages will be uploaded to the disk space provided by your Web site host. You want to make sure your host provides enough memory to store all of your pages (current and future needs), and supports online encryption. Many commercial providers will host a Web site for free (see page 68). If you are concerned about the availability of memory, technical support, and having control over page uploads, you may wish to purchase this service from a commercial provider. Fees are typically in the range of $10-20/month.

❒ *Step 3. Choose the content for your site (see Appendix D).* Integrate the availability of your store's products with this content. In addition to your store, your site might have your organization's brochure, list of board members, current and past newsletters and other publications, press releases, information about advocacy, information about new grants, financial information, information about staff members' responsibilities, news and information of use to members of the organization and the general public, and other material that will entice viewers to return again and again. You should always include contact information for the organization and the URL for the home page. You can create these pages using commercial software such as Microsoft Frontpage, which is offered by discount computer software catalogs for under $100. You can also save word processing files as HTML files, if you have a modern version of popular commercial programs. You can write your HTML code entirely in Windows Notepad. Or you can pay a commercial web developer thousands of dollars to create a custom-designed, state-of-the-art site.

❐ *Step 4. Design your site.* Decide whether you will have the site designed in-house, have it custom-built by an outside Web site developer, or use a template provided by an outside provider. Choose your options related to:

> ❐ Frames
> ❐ Fonts
> ❐ Graphics
> ❐ Animations
> ❐ Buttons
> ❐ Links
> ❐ Hit counter (see page 101)
> ❐ "Refer this page to a friend" form (see page 167)
> ❐ Site search engine (see page 166)
> ❐ Message board (see Chapter 8)
> ❐ Chat room (see Chapter 8)
> ❐ FAQ file
> ❐ Online surveys (see page 168)

Almost all of the software to create these pages can be found for free, if you are willing to accept commercial advertising in exchange.

❐ *Step 5. Consider the wording of legal notices.*

> ❐ Privacy statements (see Chapter 4)
> ❐ Codes of conduct (see Appendix G)
> ❐ Security (see Chapter 4)

❐ *Step 6. Consider other security issues.*

> ❐ Passwords and User Names
> ❐ Firewall (see Chapter 4)
> ❐ Data encryption (see Chapter 4)
> ❐ How customer data will be stored and accessed

Much of this software can be downloaded for free, but more-sophisticated versions are available commercially.

❐ *Step 7. Design the Store (see Chapter 3).*

> ❐ Create a catalog of goods you are selling.
> ❐ Set prices.

❐ Establish shipping and handling policies (see page 41).
❐ Research how to collect and remit sales taxes (see page 40).
❐ Apply for a merchant account (see page 37).
❐ Provide for a shopping cart (see page 142).
❐ Establish and publish customer service policies (see page 38).
❐ Post a Frequently Asked Questions (FAQ) file.

Perfectly suitable shopping cart software is available for free. There may be a setup charge for establishing a merchant account, plus account maintenance fees and per transaction and % of sales commissions.

❐ *Step 8. Design pages for online contributions.*

> ❐ secure form for cash
> ❐ planned giving opportunities
> ❐ in-kind donations

❐ *Step. 9. Participate in one of the new business models if you so desire (see Chapters 1, 5, and 6).*

> ❐ online charity mall
> ❐ online auction
> ❐ associate program
> ❐ payment provider
> ❐ Applications Service Provider

❐ *Step 10. Publicize your site.*

> ❐ Post news about your new site on existing electronic mailing lists.
> ❐ Establish electronic mailing lists of your own (see Appendix F).
> ❐ Advertise in publications, both online and offline, that are read by your target market.
> ❐ Put the URL for the site on everything—your stationery, business cards, newsletter, and electronic mailing lists.
> ❐ Establish a policy of periodically updating your site to encourage repeat visitors.

Marketing costs can range from virtually nothing to millions of dollars (particularly if you want a 30-second spot during the Superbowl to advertise your site, as many dot-com companies did in January 2000).

The New Social Worker online store page, accessed at: http://whitehat.safeshopper.com.
Reprinted with permission.

Chapter 3

Handling Transactions

Introduction

Nonprofit organizations that sell products and services over the Internet need to learn some new skills that for-profit business people often take for granted. Handling Internet financial transactions, managing customer service, fulfilling orders, and collecting taxes will all become routine eventually, but may seem a bit strange at first for those in the nonprofit sector. This chapter provides a short guide to some of the issues to consider when setting up an e-commerce operation.

Accepting Payment Over the Internet

Nonprofit organizations are businesses, and have many things in common with for-profit businesses. They sell products and services, such as memberships, publications, counseling, and tickets to events. They also solicit donations from the public, and it is not unusual for many donors, particularly those who have become accustomed to doing their retail shopping on the Internet, to be comfortable making these donations by credit card, either through secure forms on the Internet or conventionally. Inexorably, we are becoming a cashless society, and the public increasingly relies on credit cards for financial transactions. Nonprofit organizations should consider whether having "merchant status" is advantageous. For Web-based sales, this is a must.

Qualifying for merchant status to accept popular credit cards such as Visa, MasterCard, American Express, and Discover is often routine. An organization typically approaches its bank to set up a merchant account. You can find hundreds, if not thousands, of financial institutions willing to establish merchant accounts on the World Wide Web. One way to find them is to search under the terms "credit cards" and "merchant accounts."

Startup fees, account maintenance fees, per transaction fees, and the bank's percentage of sales commission for processing each transaction varies by financial institution, and may be negotiable. You will also need a system for transmitting the information about the transaction to the financial institution for processing, typically a terminal sold or leased by the financial institution, or computer software. The financial institution, within a few business days, credits your account for the amount of the sale after deducting transaction charges. You have to enter the card information and sales information into the terminal or software, and verify that the card is bona fide and the purchaser has not exceeded his or her credit limit. As you might expect, there is some paperwork involved, and inconvenience when a purchaser challenges a sale. On the other hand, entrepreneurial nonprofit organizations may lose out on revenue opportunities unless they satisfy the expectations of their customers.

E-cash and E-checks

For almost ten years, private firms have attempted to create technology that would permit small and large sums of money to be transferred over the Internet. One benefit of such a system is that a vendor could charge a few cents for accessing a file or using a search engine. These small amounts are not commercially viable to charge using conventional credit card technology. Other technology has been developed to permit sending checks over the Internet; the check information is sent by the customer and printed by the vendor using software provided by a private company.

In February 2000, Cybercash, Inc. announced that it had signed up its 20,000th merchant, double the number of its clients a year before. The number of transactions processed in 1999 was 57.4 million. The system permits real time online authorization of payments and settlement of transactions. Other firms, such as eCash Technologies (http://www.ecash.net) are also developing innovative electronic payment methods, and have pilot projects with internationally known banks such as Credit Suisse, Deutsche Bank, and the Bank of Austria. More than $32 million in e-cash transactions have been recorded in these pilot programs since 1994.

Within a few years, I anticipate that nonprofits with e-commerce sites will routinely be able to offer their customers an array of payment options. Commercial payment providers are hawking their services to organizations that don't want to deal with the hassles of online financial transactions, providing another option.

Customer Service

Depending on which products and services you offer, many of the issues relating to customer service will be the same for your nonprofit organization as for a for-profit. Where can I return the product for a different size? How can I get a refund? My order never arrived! Are there quantity discounts? How can I get it shipped overnight?

Most, but not all, of the reputable online shopping mall service providers have their own customer service representatives to supplement those of the merchants who participate in the mall. This is important, since you don't want your organization's telephone lines clogged up with irate customers who thought they were helping your organization by shopping, and now are not happy with your organization because of poor service provided by people with whom you have only a marginal relationship.

For those of you who are setting up your own e-commerce sites, there are several issues to consider.

The most useful page on your e-commerce Web site is likely to be your Customer Service Page's Frequently Asked Questions. The main purpose of this file is to have your customers obtain answers by viewing a file, rather than using the resources of your organization to answer them. Customers can get answers to help them solve common problems 24 hours a day, without having to make a long distance call. The FAQ file is your first line of defense against customer complaints. A second line of defense is a link to a customer service comment/complaint form. The advantages of having an electronic form is that the customer doesn't have to explain (and reexplain) the problem to your staff, perhaps being put on hold, and being given either an immediate answer that is wrong, or a correct answer that comes hours or days later. Electronic complaints are easily forwardable to the person in your organization best able to respond. As for products that your records show were shipped and the customer complains that they haven't been received, virtually every shipping company (and now, even the Post Office for some classes of mail) has a Web site that tracks packages sent by their service. It is not unusual for me to receive a tracking number from a vendor so that I, as the consumer, can track a package being shipped to me. In almost every instance, electronic customer service is less expensive than having the complaint responded to by a "live" customer service representative.

Order Fulfillment

You've successfully lured customers onto your site. They've transmitted their orders to you, and provided you with valid credit card information. How do you get the products to them?

First, you need to make sure you have enough products in stock to deliver to your customer. If you don't have a lot of inventory (or you purchase from your suppliers based on the demand), make sure your site informs the purchaser of the approximate delay they can expect between the time they make the purchase and the time the product is delivered. Next, you need to consider how the products will get to the customer. The United States Postal Service (USPS—http://new.usps.com) and United Parcel Service (UPS—http://www.ups.com) handle the bulk of packages being shipped, but there are other options, such as FedEx (http://www.fedex.com) or Airborne Express (http://www.airborne.com). Most large shipping companies provide free software to process and track shipments. Organizations can arrange for automatic pickups for a small weekly fee. Make sure you have all of the supplies you need to ship your products, such as boxes of various sizes, packing material (such as bubble wrap and filler material), shipping tape, and shipping labels.

Refund and Returns Policy

One obvious disadvantage of shopping over the Internet is that shoppers cannot touch and feel the product, or try it on or try it out. People are more willing to make purchases over the Internet when they feel that they can return the products if they are not completely satisfied. Post your refunds and returns policy on your site, and include a more liberal policy than you would expect to find at your local mall. This is good business practice, and as a nonprofit, you certainly don't want to irritate a customer who is also a donor or potential donor. Among the issues you should address are:

1. Will refunds be given in cash or credit for a future purchase?
2. How much time is permitted to elapse before returns will not be accepted?
3. Can returns be made unconditionally, or only for defective products?
4. Is there a restocking fee?
5. Must the product be returned in salable condition in the original packaging?
6. Will shipping and handling be refunded, or only the product purchase price?
7. Will your organization pay for shipping back returns?
8. Will certain products not be returnable (such as publications, electronics, or jewelry)?

Receipts and Invoices

The products should be shipped with a receipt if paid for, or an invoice if not prepaid. If not prepaid, the invoice should state the terms of payment, such as when the bill is due, and the percentage added to the bill per month for any outstanding balance. The receipt should include the name of the purchaser, the name of the organization, the description of the product(s), the price of each purchase, and the amount of tax, shipping, and handling. Generic accounting software such as Quickbooks, Quicken, MYOB Accounting or Peachtree provide forms for standard invoices and receipts.

Collecting Taxes

Only the states of Alaska, Delaware, Montana, New Hampshire, and Oregon do not have a state sales and use tax. Generally, this means that you are obligated to collect sales taxes on sales you make to customers within your state. Technically, the customer is obligated to send the sales tax to his/her state agency if from another state, although this requirement is rarely, if ever, enforced.

As a result of two U.S. Supreme Court decisions, states are not able to require remote sellers (retailers, including Internet sellers, without a physical store or warehouse or other presence in that state) to collect sales tax on sales into that state (See http://www.nga.org/106Congress/SalesTax.asp).

The Internet Tax Freedom Act (ITFA) prohibited states and local governments during a three-year moratorium (October 1, 1998-October 1, 2001) from adopting new taxes on Internet access charges. On May 10, 2000, the U.S. House of Representatives passed H.R. 3709, the Internet Nondiscrimination Act. It would extend the moratorium to October 21, 2006. If passed by the Senate and signed into law, it will eliminate Internet access taxes and fees in Texas, Wisconsin, Tennessee, South Dakota, Ohio, New Mexico, North Dakota, Montana, New Hampshire, and Washington.

Although Congress is likely to extend its moratorium against Internet sales taxes, these sales taxes still must be collected for intrastate purchases in states with sales taxes. Even if your organization is tax exempt, most states still require nonprofit organizations to collect sales taxes on sales made by them to customers within the state. Typically, states require organizations to obtain a sales tax license, and forms are provided to transmit the collected taxes to the state. It is good advice to check with a reputable local business organization, such as the Chamber of Commerce, and find out what the requirements are for collecting and transmitting state sales taxes.

Shipping and Handling

Decide how much you will charge for shipping and handling and include that information prominently on the site. Some shopping cart software provides for letting the customer decide how the product is to be shipped, and automatically adjusts the amount for shipping and handling (such as by using a database provided by your shipper), based on how much you want to add over the actual cost. You can charge a flat amount for shipping, charge by weight, charge by the number of products ordered, or provide for free shipping if the order exceeds a certain amount.

Out-of-Country Sales

Potential customers in more than 200 countries have access to your Web site. You may get orders for your products from all over the world, and you should be prepared to deal with these. Among the problems you face from foreign orders is:

1. Currency. Every country has its own form of money. You certainly don't want to receive an order in the mail for a book with a wad of rubles or kroner. The simple solution to this problem is to post a notice on your site that payment must be in U.S. dollars (credit cards automatically make the conversion). Those who buy over the Internet will know what to do to comply.

2. Shipping and handling. You certainly don't want to charge $3.50 for shipping and handling when the rate to ship a package to Botswana is $23.95. It also takes time to fill out a customs form that must be attached to the package. If you are mailing the package using the U.S. Postal Service, the package must be processed at a post office, adding to your fulfillment expense. The bottom line is that if you are willing to accept foreign orders, make it clear that an additional charge will be levied, and the customer will be notified of the amount of this charge by e-mail before the order is processed. Otherwise, put a notice on your site that makes it clear that orders can only be shipped to U.S. addresses (or to U.S. and Canadian addresses).

3. National and International Trade Laws and Sanctions. You want to make sure that you don't violate U.S. trade laws or sell to those in countries that the U.N. has levied trade sanctions against. As I write this, there are U.S. trade sanctions against a dozen countries, including Cuba, North Korea, Libya, Iraq, Serbia, Montenegro, Bosnia, UNITA (Angola), Sudan, Iran, Burma (Myanmar), Syria, and the Taliban of Afghanistan. The United States Treasury Department's Office of Foreign Assets Control (http://www.treas.gov/ofac) administers these

sanctions laws, and violations provide for criminal and civil penalties for Americans who illegally trade with hostile nations. A booklet in PDF format describing these laws and the requirements for being in compliance can be found at:

http://www.tras.gov/ofac/t11facei.pdf

Up Close:

Michael Stein—Nonprofit Technology Consultant and Author

Michael Stein is an Internet consultant based in Berkeley, CA, who works with advocacy groups, nonprofits, labor unions, and socially responsible businesses on Internet strategy, e-philanthropy, and e-commerce strategies. He is the author of two books about the Internet, including *Fundraising on the Internet: Recruiting and Renewing Donors Online* with Nick Allen and Mal Warwick. Online marketing and online fundraising are his two chief areas of specialization, and his views on the future of nonprofit e-commerce have appeared in *The Chronicle of Philanthropy* and *The Industry Standard.* Stein assists nonprofits in designing online fundraising campaigns that tie into existing events or campaigns and helps nonprofits create e-mail newsletters to communicate regularly with members and supporters. He also serves as a consultant to charities who need advice evaluating e-commerce vendors, portals, and other Internet-related service providers to make appropriate choices.

Stein is considered one of the young talents who are shaping the way nonprofits use the new technologies. His books and articles on the topic are influential in the nonprofit sector and beyond. And he is an energetic advocate for nonprofit organizations taking advantage of the new technologies available to electronically fundraise and to market their goods and services.

"Nonprofits need to pay attention to e-commerce because it is transforming society and, by the end of the decade, will be the primary means of commerce," he advises. "As computers continue to penetrate every level of the workplace, home, and civil society, and hand-held devices become familiar to all Americans, nonprofits will need to find their place in this new digital landscape."

Is it possible for nonprofits to avoid the anxiety of choosing an outside organization to develop and implement their e-commerce by doing all of the work in-house? In theory, Stein says, but most organizations need to go outside for expertise.

"I've seen groups do it themselves, if they can prioritize this as important to the organization," he says. "Professional help is going to be very useful, though. The technology is easy enough now to not require technical consultants. Of course, it helps to have an in-house champion to move things forward. Eventually, nonprofits will need a full-time Internet specialist to meet their needs."

Stein is not particularly critical of the for-profit dot-com companies who are aggressively marketing their services to nonprofits, but he points out some of the pitfalls of having a for-profit provider set up a nonprofit e-commerce site for fundraising, auctions, online malls, and/or publication sales. He feels that nonprofits should be much more communicative about their needs, rather than simply accepting all of the terms and conditions of the vendor. When organizations do go outside to find solutions, Stein feels they need to be more assertive in getting what they need and want rather than simply accepting the applications and strategies available by the vendors.

"The nonprofit organization needs to drive the relationship with the vendor to assure that their needs are met," he contends. "It's equally important that the for-profit provider understand the specific needs of the nonprofit, and be responsive and flexible. It's not just about 'customer relationships' and 'product placement.' "

Stein has seen firsthand how charities have recorded significant accomplishments in using the Internet to raise funds to support their worthy missions, funds that may have otherwise gone undonated.

"From personal experience, Children Now (www.childrennow.org) had a great success working with www.Adam.com when the latter was doing a 'Doc Around the Clock,' a 24-hour online event where a physician answered questions online. Children Now was one of four charities that received $5 each time someone entered the event. It raised $3,000 in 24 hours," he applauds. "A success factor was publicity and a creative partnership between the nonprofit and the for-profit."

Despite the technological and marketing sophistication of Children Now, the organization hasn't been able to raise money through charity malls. The lesson learned by Children Now is one Stein believes all organizations in the voluntary sector should take to heart.

"It doesn't fit Children Now's donor profile to encourage people to shop for charity," he observes. "It also required too much publicity work on Children Now's behalf to promote the charity mall. It's important the fit be right and also important to know when to pull the plug on something that isn't working and is wasting time."

Stein offers the following advice to nonprofit organizations who are just beginning to test the waters on selling products and services on their Web sites, and using the Internet to raise funds.

"Stay focused on a few e-commerce items that can tie into the nonprofit's mission," he counsels. "Concentrate your e-commerce campaign in two annual drives that coincide with events or campaigns that the organization is engaged in. Find for-profit or corporate partners to assist with outreach and publicity. And use this effort as an excuse to get more people involved in your organization by finding volunteers to help."

Generally, Stein is very optimistic that the Internet will provide a powerful forum for organizations to build lasting relationships with new donors, and communicate more information with lower costs and more quickly than by conventional methods.

"Nonprofits have a unique ability to build community with their donors, supporters, and friends," he points out. "It's critical to not lose sight of this. So far, I think most nonprofits realize this. In the next few years, that challenge will grow greater."

Where does Stein side on the debate on whether charities should consider sending unsolicited e-mails to millions of recipients in the hope of receiving a few donations? He's squarely within the consensus against engaging in the practice of sending indiscriminate bulk e-mail, but favors using e-mail to communicate with those who already have a relationship with the organization.

"I don't think there's anything fundamentally unethical about sending e-mail spam," he expresses. "After all, nonprofits have been buying mailing lists and sending out bulk mail solicitation letters for over two decades. With the modern practice of e-mail spam, though, it's reached new heights of annoyance to the recipients and will generally waste the nonprofit's time and energy. There will soon be a consumer backlash against e-mail spam, including laws that restrict its use. Nonprofits ought to use e-mail aggressively and intelligently to communicate with their opt-in supporters and audiences, but stay away from buying lists from list brokers."

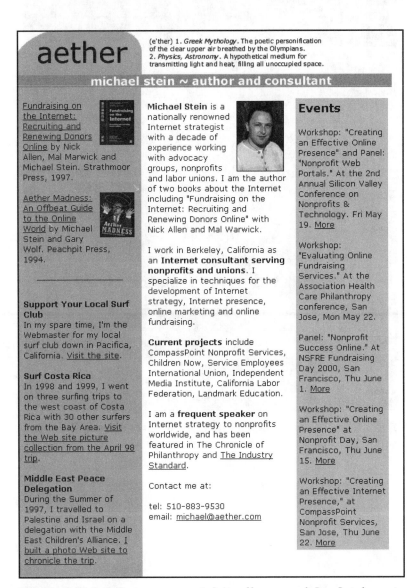

aether

(e'ther) 1. *Greek Mythology*. The poetic personification of the clear upper air breathed by the Olympians. 2. *Physics, Astronomy*. A hypothetical medium for transmitting light and heat, filling all unoccupied space.

michael stein ~ author and consultant

Fundraising on the Internet: Recruiting and Renewing Donors Online by Nick Allen, Mal Marwick and Michael Stein. Strathmoor Press, 1997.

Aether Madness: An Offbeat Guide to the Online World by Michael Stein and Gary Wolf. Peachpit Press, 1994.

Support Your Local Surf Club
In my spare time, I'm the Webmaster for my local surf club down in Pacifica, California. Visit the site.

Surf Costa Rica
In 1998 and 1999, I went on three surfing trips to the west coast of Costa Rica with 30 other surfers from the Bay Area. Visit the Web site picture collection from the April 98 trip.

Middle East Peace Delegation
During the Summer of 1997, I travelled to Palestine and Israel on a delegation with the Middle East Children's Alliance. I built a photo Web site to chronicle the trip.

Michael Stein is a nationally renowned Internet strategist with a decade of experience working with advocacy groups, nonprofits and labor unions. I am the author of two books about the Internet including "Fundraising on the Internet: Recruiting and Renewing Donors Online" with Nick Allen and Mal Warwick.

I work in Berkeley, California as an **Internet consultant serving nonprofits and unions**. I specialize in techniques for the development of Internet strategy, Internet presence, online marketing and online fundraising.

Current projects include CompassPoint Nonprofit Services, Children Now, Service Employees International Union, Independent Media Institute, California Labor Federation, Landmark Education.

I am a **frequent speaker** on Internet strategy to nonprofits worldwide, and has been featured in The Chronicle of Philanthropy and The Industry Standard.

Contact me at:

tel: 510-883-9530
email: michael@aether.com

Events

Workshop: "Creating an Effective Online Presence" and Panel: "Nonprofit Web Portals." At the 2nd Annual Silicon Valley Conference on Nonprofits & Technology. Fri May 19. More

Workshop: "Evaluating Online Fundraising Services." At the Association Health Care Philanthropy conference, San Jose, Mon May 22.

Panel: "Nonprofit Success Online." At NSFRE Fundraising Day 2000, San Francisco, Thu June 1. More

Workshop: "Creating an Effective Online Presence" at Nonprofit Day, San Francisco, Thu June 15. More

Workshop: "Creating an Effective Internet Presence," at CompassPoint Nonprofit Services, San Jose, Thu June 22. More

Michael Stein's home page at: http://www. michaelstein.net.
Reprinted with permission.

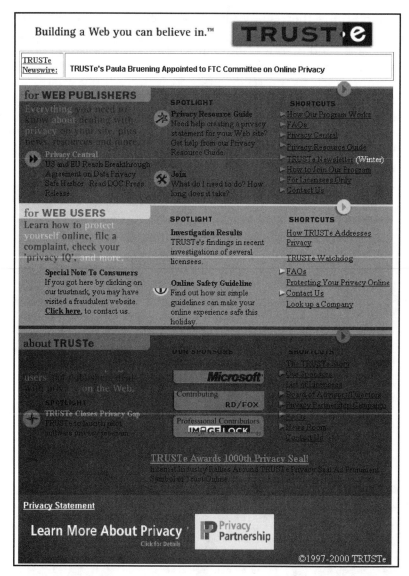

The TRUSTe home page at http://www.Truste.org. Reprinted with permission.

Chapter 4

Security, Privacy, and Other Issues

Introduction

Even putting e-commerce transactions aside, nonprofit organizations have lots of reasons to protect the security and privacy of the computer files they generate and the communications they send over the Internet. Human service organizations, for example, routinely use client files which, if disclosed in an unauthorized manner, could cause irreparable harm to their clients and could result in lawsuits. E-mail exchanges may involve sensitive personnel matters or contract negotiations with unions and other entities. Even if nothing sensitive is discussed in a file or e-mail message, you still do not want any nosy person, within your organization or outside of it, to be able to browse through your business.

For most businesses, privacy is second nature. How many businesses send out communications discussing business matters using postcards or unsealed letters? Our guess is that if they did so, most of these communications would never be read, other than by their intended targets. But we have peace of mind believing that when we put a letter in an envelope and seal it, the letter will reach its destination without being read by someone else.

E-commerce transactions provide yet another reason for nonprofits to be concerned about Internet security and privacy. Fortunately, concerns about both are being addressed by software that is readily available for free or for a nominal charge.

Copyright infringement, trademark infringement, and unrelated business taxes (UBIT) are among some of the other issues nonprofits need to be concerned about when they set up an e-commerce site. As with security and privacy, these issues remain unsettled.

SSL and Other Encryption Technology

Virtually every survey has demonstrated the pervasive fear of consumers with respect to providing their credit card numbers over the Internet. The concern that unscrupulous merchants (or those who pretend to be merchants) will use the credit card information is mostly unfounded; even if this happened (and it does occasionally), there are limits on the amount of loss the consumer sustains (typically $50), and there is no exposure to loss if the problem is reported promptly. The principal concern tends to be that hackers will somehow tap into the transaction and steal the credit card data. It is probably a more likely occurrence that credit card data is stolen simply as a result of people, both merchants and consumers, being careless with the paper records of these transactions. Nonetheless, a lot of effort has gone into making financial transactions over the Internet safe by encrypting (that is, disguising) the data so that only the intended sender and receiver can read it.

While there are several protocols for encryption, the industry standard for e-commerce has become Secure Sockets Layer, or SSL. SSL was created by Netscape and is a feature of the company's browser. The Netscape program uses what's known as a public and private key system and the use of a digital certificate.

Without having both the public and private keys, a message that is encrypted looks like gobbledygook. Each person has his or her own private key, which is kept very secret, and a public key, which is shared with everyone. The messages cannot be read without having both. Thus if you send an encrypted message to someone and use their public key, you cannot even read the encrypted message yourself because you don't have access to their private key.

Two popular encryption programs are available. PGP, or Pretty Good Privacy, can be found at http://www.pgp.com. It can be downloaded for commercial use for a modest fee. A similar program that does not use sophisticated algorithms that are subject to Department of Commerce export restrictions has also been developed. GnuPG is available for free at the following site: http://www.gnupg.org.

There is an excellent Web site that explains encryption in more detail at:

http://hotwired.lycos.com/webmonkey/backend/security

Certification/Authentication

If you will be serious about e-commerce on your site, you should consider obtaining a server certificate from a certifying authority to assure purchasers that you are who you say you are. A purchaser can see something on their browser that authenticates your encryption software if you have one of these certificates. Many people will refuse to send their credit card information over the Internet unless you have a valid certificate. Server certificates are available commercially from many different companies, and the cost varies. Some freeware includes a certificate, but there may be problems using free versions on some browsers.

The most widely used authority in the United States is VeriSign (see page 164).   Competing companies include Thawte Consulting (http://www.thawte.com), Entrust (http://www.entrust.com); GTE CyberTrust (http://www.cybertrust.gte.com; EuroSign (http://eurosign.com); COST (http://www.cost.se; Binary Surgeons (http://www.surgeons.co.za/certificate.html); and Keywitness (http://www.keywitness.ca). One recurring problem is that the certificates may not work on all browsers, so make sure to inquire about this information.

Digital Signatures

On June 30, 2000, President Bill Clinton signed into law The Electronic Signatures in Global and National Commerce Act. The purpose of this law is to give electronically signed documents the same legal status under federal law as documents signed on paper. Such electronic signatures have been legalized in at least 40 states. The digital signature works the same way as the digital certificates, using encryption with public and private keys stored on the user's hard drive or on a smart card, similar to that used by the President to sign the bill into law. (He also signed the bill using a conventional pen.)

Protection of Customer Data

You can have all of the sophisticated encryption systems in place, but it won't do any good if you keep the printouts on your desk, or put them in an accessible file on your computer that is not password-protected. Take reasonable precautions to keep your customer data protected.

Firewalls

A firewall is a term that describes Internet security software that limits access to your site from the Internet, allowing approved traffic in and out through a secure gateway. Firewalls can be downloaded free from the Internet (for example, find one at: http://edge.fireplug.net/) or can be obtained for thousands of dollars. See http://www.interhack.net/pubs/fwfaq/ for a complete guide to firewalls. For the technically inclined, point your browser to http://www.ntresearch.com/firewall.htm for more on the technical details of how they work and strategies for building your Web site's security defensive perimeter.

Privacy Policies

Every other day or so, I get a spam e-mail encouraging me to pay $24.95 for software that will access Internet databases. With this software, I supposedly should be able to access unlisted telephone numbers, criminal records, driving records, and "Get anyone's name and address with just a license plate number (Find that girl you met in traffic!)." I haven't purchased this product (I won't, as a general principal, have any transaction with a company that markets by using spam e-mail). But I have little doubt that many, if not all, of its claims are true. I am not yet at the point that I fear that a lot of data is being collected on me and my family for criminal or other mischievous purposes. But I recognize that a lot of personal information is being collected about me, the products I buy, and the Web sites I visit. Once it is in some database, I have no control over how this database is used, including how and when the data are transferred to a third party without my knowledge and consent.

As more people become comfortable with making purchases over the Internet, there will be less fear over disclosing credit card information online. Personally, I would rather give out my credit card number over a secure commercial site than to a store clerk. Our culture is such that many Americans mistrust businesses, and they are less willing to do business online if they do not trust the business organization.

Many commercial Web sites address the privacy concern by having a privacy policy posted online. The policy generally includes—

1. What information will be shared with others, and under what circumstances. For example, many organizations sell or rent their mailing lists.

2. What information will not be shared with others. For example, a telephone number is required to provide verification of a credit card. While many business organizations will request the telephone number for that purpose (or to communicate with the customer in the event there is a problem with the transaction), they will keep the customer's telephone number confidential.

3. What customers can do to keep their name and address confidential. This may entail simply clicking a box on an electronic form.

TRUSTe is an organization that was established to set up privacy standards and provide sanctions against participants who violate the standards. Web sites that meet TRUSTe's strict privacy standards in the areas of notice, choice, access, and security and which submit to TRUSTe's oversight program can display the organization's seal. It has become the Web privacy equivalent of the "Good Housekeeping Seal of Approval." The fee ranges from $299 for organizations with annual revenue of up to $1 million, $599 for those with $5-$10 million, to $1,999 for those with revenues of between $10 and $25 million. For more information, visit the TRUSTe Trademark Web site at: http://www.truste.org.

Cookies

One feature of the Internet that has contributed to fears about privacy violation is the cookie. The cookie feature was created by Netscape as part of its browser. Cookies are ASCII files (plain text) that can be created and accessed by a Web site visited by the browser. The file is resident in the browser directory, so if you decide to use another browser, the cookie won't be readable by the originating Web site. You can also delete your cookies or disable the browser feature that creates them. The benefit of the feature is that the cookie file lets the site you are visiting know something about you and your interests by accessing it, and permits the site to provide custom-designed information based on your cookie. Having a cookie can save you a lot of time and keystrokes, because the site will "recognize" you as a repeat visitor and "remember" what you did on previous visits. The downside is that you may not wish to share this information. For a more detailed look at the pros and cons of cookies, visit The Unofficial Cookie FAQ at: http://www.cookiecentral.com/faq.

Copyrights

Nonprofit managers who use the Internet need to be concerned about the copyright laws for plenty of reasons. First, nonprofit organizations post lots of materials on their Web pages that they don't necessarily want to see reproduced and disseminated without their permission. Second, nonprofit managers use a lot of material they find on the World Wide Web, which may or may not be copyrighted. It is important to have an understanding of how these materials may be legally used. Third, nonprofit managers send e-mail and post messages to electronic news groups and mailing lists. It may make a difference how you word something if you know that a publisher can include as a direct quote in a book with a 100,000 first printing something that you innocently posted on a Usenet group.

Copyright law changes all of the time, based on how individual cases are decided by the courts. Nothing in this section is intended to be legal advice; even if the information here and in Appendix B, *A Short Course in Copyright Law*, is correct at the time of publication, the information can change. And some of this material is an interpretation of statutes and case-law that many legal scholars would feel comfortable refuting. When in doubt, consult a qualified attorney.

Several Web sites keep up with Internet controversies involving what has been labeled "intellectual property"—patents, trademarks, and copyrights. Among the better sites are: U.S. Copyright Office (http://lcweb.loc.gov/copyright/) and the Institute for Learning Technologies at Columbia University (http://www.ilt.columbia.edu/text_version/projects/copyright/ILTcopy1.html).

See Appendix B for *A Short Course on Copyright Issues*.

Trademarks

Trademarks and service marks are legal protection afforded to words and symbols that identify a product or service in a way that is intended to distinguish them from the goods and services of others. Federal law provides for registration of trademarks used in commerce. Trademarks are acquired as a result of the first use of a valid mark in commerce. No registration is required, although registration, of course, assists those who claim an infringement. Those who register their trademarks are entitled to use a symbol "®" after the mark. Registration applications are not automatically approved by the Patent and Trademark Office. Examining attorneys consider whether the word or phrase is already in common use and therefore ineligible, or if the mark is confusingly similar to another already registered. The fee is currently $325 for each application, and you can apply for a trademark online at:

http://www.uspto.gov/teas/index.html

The full details can be obtained over the Internet from the Web site of the U.S. Department of Commerce's Patent and Trademark Office:

http://www.uspto.gov

For additional information on this topic, point your browser to:

http://www.eff.org/pub/Intellectual_property/

Federal Unrelated Business Income Tax (UBIT)

If your organization sells goods and services on its Web site or accepts commercial advertising, you may need to become familiar with laws and regulations governing unrelated business income taxes (UBIT). Federal law provides that nonprofit corporations must pay federal taxes on unrelated business income. Corporations with at least $1,000 of such income are required to file a 990-T annually. Income is defined as unrelated if it is derived from a trade or business, is regularly carried on, and is substantially unrelated to the exempt purpose of the corporation. Income clearly exempt from UBIT includes that generated from activities performed by volunteers, that from selling merchandise received as gifts or contributions, and dividends, interest, royalties and capital gains. Also exempt is income from business operations that are conducted for the "convenience" of an organization's members, students, patients, and staff, such as a hospital cafeteria or college bookstore.

The Internal Revenue Service reports that $502 million in UBIT was collected from 50,034 organizations in 1996, and $486 million was collected from 48,563 organizations in 1997.

The Internal Revenue Service has aggressively audited some charities focusing on UBIT issues, and has taken charities to court to promote its policy of restricting UBIT exemptions. During the 1990s, the Internal Revenue Service expanded its attention to enforcement of UBIT, and developed policies with respect to some of the gray areas that were problematic to charities. Some cases involving the interpretation of what constitutes unrelated income were litigated. Several relatively recent decisions on generic UBIT issues have been decided in favor of charities. Three examples have been cases involving mailing list rental income, affinity credit card income, and income from bingo games.

Two cases involving whether mailing list rental income is considered subject to UBIT have resulted in victories for the challenged charity. The first involved the Sierra Club, which was heard by the 9th Circuit Court of Appeals. A subsequent case before United States Tax Court involving the American Academy of Ophthalmology also found that such income was not taxable. Tax Court also rejected the contention of the IRS that payments made to the Mississippi State University Alumni Association by a bank were royalty payments rather than business income, and thus are not subject to UBIT. Each of these three cases had fact-specific aspects that may not apply to every case of a charity generating revenues by renting its mailing list or utilizing an affinity credit card arrangement, and some caution needs to be taken in generalizing. However, the courts apparently been have reining in the IRS for a generally broad interpretation of what constitutes unrelated business income, and this is a positive trend for charities seeking unconventional methods to generate the revenue they need to provide their services. A third case, involving income from instant pull-tab bingo games, developed when the IRS determined that income from these games conducted by Women of the Motion Picture Industry and other 501(c)(3) and (c)(6) organizations was subject to UBIT. The tax code does provide for UBIT exception for most bingo game income, but the conditions are narrow and do not apply to the instant pull-tab games. Tax Court ruled in favor of the organizations.

A case decided August 1996 in U.S. District Court involving the American Academy of Family Physicians decided that the organization's income from a group insurance plan offered to its members underwritten by a private insurance carrier was not subject to UBIT. Again, the facts of this case may not be typical of conventional agreements between an insurance carrier and an exempt organization, but the opinion of the court on the issue was a favorable development.

Latest UBIT Development from the IRS

In February 2000, the Internal Revenue Service promulgated a draft regulation addressing the issue of corporate sponsorships of charitable events. Currently, the tax code (Section 513(i)) makes a distinction between "qualified sponsorship payments," and payments for advertising or other services. The first type is generally not subject to UBIT, although the second type generally is. Under this provision, an exempt organization must treat as taxable income any portion of a payment from a corporate donor that is received in exchange for a "substantial return benefit," unless such payments would be exempt under traditional principles applying to UBIT. For example, if a payment for a substantial return benefit falls under one of the exclusions from UBIT found in Section 512(b), which include dividends, interest, rents from real property, and royalties, it would not be taxable.

The issue addressed by the new regulation is what constitutes such a benefit, and provides a "safe harbor" for some of these benefits. The IRS does not consider it to be taxable if an organization merely posts the logo of the sponsoring company at the event. The gray area is what happens, for example, when the logo is on the charity's Web site, and links to the Web site of the sponsoring company? Is this merely "advertising" rather than charitable sponsorship?

"Organizations must make a good faith estimate of the portion of a sponsorship payment allocable to taxable services. Section 513(i) provides explicitly that a single sponsorship payment may include both taxable and nontaxable components, depending on the portion of the payment that reflects services rendered," explains Lloyd H. Mayer of the Washington-based law firm of Caplin & Drysdale. "The proposed regulations reflect this allocation principle, but impose on the exempt organization the burden of determining the fair market value of the taxable benefits provided to the sponsor. If the organization cannot establish that the payment exceeds the fair value of the benefits—including any exclusive provider arrangement—then the entire payment will be taxable. Under a new anti-abuse provision, segregating the provision of taxable benefits and nontaxable acknowledgments into separate written agreements will apparently not prevent the IRS from treating the two transactions as one for purposes of determining whether any portion of sponsor's payments exceeds the value of the services it receives."

Up Close: Putnam Barber

Evergreen Society President

Putnam Barber teaches in the MPA program of the Institute of Public Service at Seattle University and serves on the Visiting Committee for the Master in Not-for-Profit Leadership Program there. He is a Senior Advisor to the Internet ASP company Social Ecology and a columnist for the *Chronicle of Philanthropy.* He is a frequent speaker on nonprofit issues and a frequent contributor to electronic mailing lists such as the Gilbert Center's Nonprofit Fundraising, CharityChannel's CyberGifts, and Harriet Bograd's Cyber-Accountability. *The Non-Profit Times* included Barber in its list of the 50 most influential people in the nonprofit sector.

Barber is a fervent advocate for nonprofit organizations exploring how e-commerce and e-philanthropy can help them achieve their charitable missions.

"Because e-commerce is increasingly the model by which business is done, organizations that can't master e-commerce will find their activities increasingly marginalized," Barber points out. "That being said, e-commerce offers significant cost savings over other forms of commerce and also offers significant revenue opportunities."

Where should one begin?

"I strongly believe there's no substitute for the first step of just trying it," he recommends. "Visit helping.org and make a donation to an organization you already support. Surf the web, looking for organizations you believe in, and see what they offer in the way of e-commerce on their Web sites. Explore one of the lively charity shopping sites such as iGive.com or GreaterGood.com and buy something with the proceeds earmarked for an organization you like. Look up your own organization through Guidestar and see what diligent 'net surfers are already learning about what you do and how. Two or three hours spent exploring in this way will give a sense of the possibilities and inspire more questions than seemed possible at the start.

"As a second step, I suggest hiring a coach—preferably someone from outside the organization—or commissioning a project involving people from several departments charged with offering recommendations about a responsible development path," he continues. "Some explorers may want to 'lurk' to read the discussions on the e-lists that focus on these topics. That's a good way to absorb ideas and develop challenges for one's own organization's future. Others will want to attend conferences and training sessions on these subjects; they are offered frequently throughout the country."

Barber recommends that decision-makers expect to hear from opposing camps, respectively arguing for alacrity and caution.

"Some folks will be skeptical and full of dire warnings of totally unreasonable expense and others will breezily dismiss the difficulties and the risks while urging immediate action. Both these postures are simply wrong," he says. "Every nonprofit needs to be charting a course toward using the power of the Internet to aid it in its work—raising money, delivering services, building relationships. And every nonprofit needs to balance the costs and distractions of doing that against all the other demands on limited resources of skill, money, and attention."

What does Putnam think about the potential of the Internet to provide a windfall in donations to worthy charities and spark a renaissance of philanthropy?

"I don't believe the Internet will ever be a reliable source of 'free money from strangers,' " he predicts. "Anticipating that sort of windfall will lead only to disappointment for most organizations. Spending money to build a program with that as the goal will just add embarrassment."

But that is no excuse for not getting on board and beginning to develop a sensible e-philanthropy and e-commerce strategy for your organization, he says. What should you be doing now?

"First, look among your current supporters for people who will adapt easily to using the 'net to support your cause. It's quick, simple, and inexpensive – or at least it should be. Some supporters may welcome e-philanthropy because it's easier for them. Some may be attracted to the savings it offers you. If you do things right for the early adopters, it is very likely larger proportions of your supporters will embrace the efforts in short order.

"Second, look for things you already do that can be digitized in ways that will streamline operations and reduce costs. If you create an annual fundraising calendar with illustrations related to your program, make a digital copy and put it online. A donor can download a copy to print on a color copier with a few clicks. Out-of-pocket cost? A few cents for the credit card transaction fee. No inventory. No shipping. No issues with processing small payments.

"Third, imagine ways people in far-away places can relate to what you do. For many organizations, this may be a matter of building a way to maintain the loyalties of the 20% of American households that move every year. The difficulty and expense of staying in touch with supporters who move away is genuinely daunting—if it's done on the phone or through the mails. Too often, any such efforts degenerate into little more than appeals for funds—addressed without much hope to people who rapidly lose whatever reasons they had to give. Extending your e-mail and Web presentations the extra distance needed to maintain connections with far-away supporters may require relatively small additions to what would be done anyway, and yield both program and financial benefits for the organizations that make the effort."

While credible DIY (Do-It-Yourself) e-commerce sites are on the Web, Barber recommends that organizations consider tapping professional expertise for designing their e-commerce sites. "As an addicted Internet user, I see way too much stuff that is simply bad —out of date, transparently inaccurate, clumsily designed, and incompetently slapped together," he complains. "The tools for avoiding such damaging presentations are readily available and easily mastered by nonprofit staff. Developing the strategy, identifying the tools, and structuring operations, though, depends on knowledge of a range of choices and complexities of integration. When nonprofit people are committed to their mission, they don't have time to master these complexities. Time spent identifying a trustworthy consultant will be quickly repaid as the agency's Internet activities mature."

What are some of the factors that result in charities being successful in using the Internet to fundraise? Barber points out several.

"Clarity of mission and need are perhaps the most important factors in online fundraising success," he judges. "Add to that a well-known brand with unimpeachable integrity, and a consistent presentation in all media on stationery, in print materials, and e-mail communications. With that in mind, it is no surprise that the American Red Cross is breaking all records for e-philanthropy."

He also sees some patterns with failures as well. "NetAid (see page 60) is a classic example of a failure, though some real money was in fact raised," he acknowledges. "The whole project was technology and sales driven. The sponsors' motives were transparently focused on proving their capacity to handle multiple simultaneous connections, with donations being an afterthought. The sponsors were guilty of clumsy fundraising. Neither the ultimate recipients nor the decision-making apparatus was in place on the day of the concerts."

Barber also feels that other problems contributed to the meager results of NetAid. "The site had poor Web design, making it difficult to navigate to the donation page, and it was unclear how the process worked. In a way, the fact that NetAid raised any money at all is a strong testament to the potential power of online fundraising—we might have expected it to accomplish absolutely nothing, when in fact more than a million dollars in new donations went to the United Nations Development program and other causes once the board was organized."

Barber has been a vocal critic of utilizing e-mail messages sent to strangers, or spam, for fundraising purposes, although he acknowledges that there are credible reports that it can be done profitably in at least some charitable contexts.

"When one organization annoys thousands, maybe even millions, of e-mail readers in pursuit of the possibility of a handful of donations from a tiny fraction of recipients, every nonprofit's chance to build a relationship with those millions is impaired," he charges. "It is a classic example of polluting the commons, translated into the environment of cyberspace. As with most forms of pollution, the damage done by spamming is hard to discern in any one case, unpredictable, and cumulative. Unlike the people who leave old mattresses in out-of-the-way corners of parks, though, it is easy to identify spammers. An important defense is for the rest of us to have a harshly unforgiving attitude and long memories."

"Of course, the need to find new donors is a fact of life for all nonprofits that depend on public support," he says. "E-mail is a low-cost way of communicating and imposes only slight inconveniences on its recipients, especially if it is done 'gently'—using brief plain-text messages and candid subject lines. There's no doubt that spam is widely detested. But does strong negative energy surrounding a particular method of fundraising make it unethical? If so, then telemarketing is probably a greater ethical lapse than spam."

He adds that spam may have worse consequences for organizations that misuse e-mail, though. For example, people who are technologically savvy and strongly spam-averse may set their e-mail filters to discard all incoming e-mail from a spamming charity. "Once people set filters that way," he points out, "a charity that wants to re-open e-mail contact will find it difficult, expensive, perhaps even impossible to do."

Barber is viewed by many as one of the most influential Third Sector philosophers, thinkers, and futurists. As you can see from his comments on the subject, he is bullish on the future of nonprofit e-commerce and e-philanthropy, and isn't shy about sharing his provocative views with an audience that is increasingly warming to his vision of the nonprofit community.

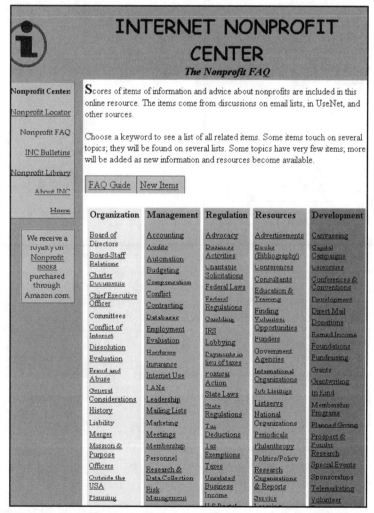

The Nonprofit FAQ Page at: http://www.nonprofits. org/npofaq. Reprinted with permission.

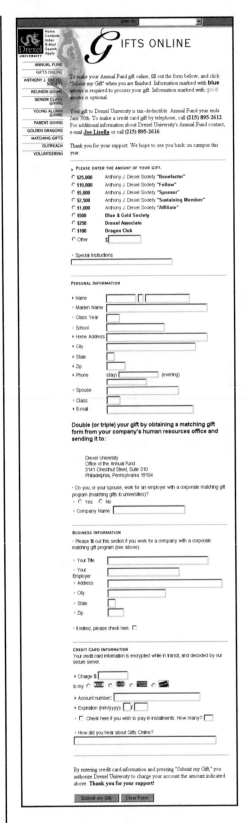

The Drexel University online gifts page at http://www.drexel.edu/ia/onlinegifts. Reprinted with permission.

Chapter 5

Fundraising on the Internet

Introduction

Not much is known about how much money charities are raising using the Internet. However, a study published in the June 15, 2000 issue of the *Chronicle of Philanthropy* provides evidence that the amount of money donated via organization Web sites is increasing. This survey of 252 of the largest charities in the United States found that only slightly more than a third of them raised any money at all on the Internet, and just 11 reported raising more than $100,000 in 1999. Forty percent of the $7 million total reported raised over the Internet was by the American Red Cross. A minimal amount, perhaps $150,000, was raised by these charities through charity portals described beginning on page 148. The study also provided evidence of something that was suspected before—many of those who are contributing online to a charity are first-time contributors to that charity and were not previously in the charity's database of potential contributors.

A 1999 study by the Arlington, VA-based direct marketing and fundraising firm Craver, Matthews, Smith & Co. (http://www.craveronline.com) found that 50 million American adults are online and report giving time or money to social causes. Two-thirds of them say that they haven't heard anything from their favorite charities about opportunities to interact with them online, and just 7% reported making an online donation. An oft-quoted statistic originated by Mark Rovner, a senior vice president of Craver, Matthews, Smith & Co., estimates that just 14 cents of every $100 donated to charity in 1999 was donated online.

This can be interpreted in two ways. The first is that online giving is an almost insignificant proportion of the way Americans give, and thus is not worthy of too much attention from nonprofit organization advocates. The second is that the potential for online giving has not begun to be tapped.

I'm a strong advocate for the second interpretation. If one looks at the growth of the Internet for conducting business transactions, particularly the explosion in online retailing, there is reason to believe that this second interpretation is justified. American consumers are buying online, and becoming comfortable with using their credit cards to do so. As the number who do so increases, I predict that the number who will donate to charities using the same method will also increase, until it reaches the point at which online giving, in one model or another, will become the dominant method of giving. It might take ten years or it might take forty years, but I believe it will happen. There are signs today of the unlimited potential of using the Internet for fundraising.

Success Stories

In just a single day in August 1999, the American Red Cross raised almost $140,000 online for earthquake disaster victims in Izmil, Turkey. That charity, based in Arlington, Virginia, is often cited in reports about Internet fundraising successes. More than $1 million was raised through Internet donations for its Kosovo relief program in April 1999. In the fiscal year that ended June 30, 1998, just $170,000 was raised on the Red Cross Web site. That figure grew to $2.5 million the following year.

Catholic Relief Services raised nearly that much online, 10% of the amount the organization raised as a result of its direct mail solicitation.

The Salvation Army raised $150,000 from its Web site donation button in its first four months of being placed on its Web pages, beginning in October 1999.

World Vision raised more than a half-million dollars in 1999 over the Internet, and about 4,000 children have been sponsored by online donors in the three years that the organization has had a Web presence.

New York NPR affiliate WNYC raised $148,000 online during the first six months of 1999, compared to just $20,000 online for the entire previous year.

Goodwill Industries reported that it raised $315,000 in just nine months from its online charity auctions.

Not all charities have fared as well. NetAid, a charity that sponsored a series of Internet concert broadcasts to raise funds for world hunger relief, set up a Web site prepared to handle a million hits per minute, hundreds of millions of potential donors per concert. Even after being endorsed by President Bill Clinton, Prime Minister Tony Blair, and Nelson Mandela, only about a million dollars were raised from the public from the 2.5 million viewers who heard all or some of the broadcast, a fraction of the money invested in the project by its corporate sponsors, Cisco Systems and KPMG. World-wide negative publicity followed for the charity.

Charity Portals

Scores of for-profit and nonprofit dot-com companies are sprouting up, promising donors to take donations over the Internet by credit card, and funneling the donation, sometimes after deducting an administrative fee, to the charity. For charities that receive an unsolicited check in the mail from one of these portal companies, this is a windfall. For the donor, this can also be a convenience, and it often provides donor anonymity if requested. The donor can use the site search engine to find a suitable charity, and there is often other content on the portal site to influence donation decisions. For the commercial vendor, the administrative fee pays the bills and provides a profit. Some make money by selling advertising on their sites. Others charge charities to be listed.

Some of these portals may not be legitimate. Many others are, but it is difficult to tell which are and which are not simply by visiting the Web site. To the best of my knowledge, no one has systematically investigated which sites deliver on their promises.

For many charities, being listed on these portals is a way to publicize the existence of the organization and the importance of its mission, even if donations received from participation are minimal. For others, being associated with a firm that takes a commission on donations is unacceptable. According to a report that appeared in the *Chronicle of Philanthropy*, the World Wildlife Fund sent "cease and desist" letters threatening to take legal action unless the sites did not remove the name of the organization from the list of organizations eligible to receive donations from the portals.

As I write this, most of the portal sites are less than two years old and have little track record. The Internal Revenue Service has raised questions about whether donations made through these portals can be deductible for federal income tax purposes. Many are not likely to survive, since it takes a lot of marketing capital to draw people to the site and donate. In general, sites that require the charity to pay any kind of upfront fee are likely to be a scam. There are portals, such as Helping.org (affiliated with America Online), that provide the entire donation to designated charities, and pay transaction costs out of a foundation. How all of this will shake out is anybody's guess, but as more and more charities build their own Web sites that routinely accept donations by secure credit card forms, donations made through portals are likely to be a small part of the online donation calculus.

Use of Spam

Anyone with an e-mail account knows firsthand the annoyance of receiving unsolicited, bulk e-mail message selling products, offering "get rich quick" schemes, and promoting smut Web sites. A spirited debate on the Online Fundraising electronic mailing list frequented by fundraisers and others associated with nonprofit organizations in May 2000 focused on the pros and cons (mostly cons) of using the Internet to send unsolicited fundraising solicitations to millions of personal computer e-mail accounts. There was, as one might expect, professional curiosity about whether sending spam e-mail raised more money than was required to finance the fundraising effort. But I got the impression that even if there were success stories, few, if any, of the participants would engage in this behavior, which most felt violated ethical principles.

Yet despite an almost universal disdain for fundraisers who send out spam, almost everyone felt that it was desirable to send e-mail to those with a prior connection to the organization to tell them about giving opportunities.

I agree, and here are nine reasons why charities should avoid sending spam messages as a fundraising technique.

Nine reasons not to spam:

1. Harvesting e-mails using software is time-consuming. It takes time to eliminate duplicates and to babysit the computer so it doesn't freeze up midway through the process of broadcasting the messages.

2. Almost all Internet Service Providers don't permit sending spam. They can and will cancel your account.

3. A large amount of undeliverable mail and unwanted mail (such as return spam, irate complaints, and copies of complaints to your ISP) is returned back to your e-mail box.

4. Many people pay to receive their e-mail outside of the U.S., and many in the U.S. still pay for incremental hours of Internet service, including those who travel and are accessing their e-mail through a hotel or airport account or when using an Internet café.

5. The cost of unwanted e-mail, in both time and money, falls on the recipient, not the sender. There is no incentive for the sender to delete the e-mail address, compared to the sender of unwanted snail mail communications.

6. Unwanted e-mail adds to the fear, real or imagined, that the communication may harbor viruses, worms, or Trojan horses.

7. Most everyone considers spam to be obnoxious and annoying. Other types of communications have remedies available to register complaints or filter out communications, such as caller I.D., or returning mail to the post office marked "refused."

8. Spamming may soon become illegal. Legislation (H.R. 3113, the *Unsolicited Electronic Mail Act of 2000*) was reported out by the House Commerce Committee's Subcommittee on Telecommunications, Trade and Consumer Protection in March 2000. It would require spam to be labeled, permit ISPs to prohibit customers from sending spam, and permit ISPs to sue spammers who violate such a prohibition. Similar legislation is also pending in the Senate.

9. The dominant reason not to send fundraising spam is that regardless of whether it is practical or cost-effective for the charity, it violates the spirit of the Internet and the values inherent in the charitable sector.

Regulation of Internet Fundraising

Currently, only 10 states do not regulate charitable solicitation. Many of those with registration and reporting requirements have adopted a model state law. Thirty-one states and the District of Columbia accept a standardized Unified Registration Statement (URS), although six of these states require an additional supplemental form.

Almost every state law defines charitable solicitation in a manner that includes under its aegis donation requests made from an organizational Web site. Yet regulating Internet donations poses a practical quandary for both the regulator and the charity, particularly the small charity. First, how can a state enforce its solicitation law on a small charity in another state that might not be targeting out-of-state donors, but may simply have a donation page on its Web site that is accessible to the entire Internet community?

Courts have consistently ruled that the states have a legitimate interest in assuring that donors have access to information about the charities to which they might donate, permitting the states to monitor the activities of those organizations that are generally granted favorable treatment compared to for-profit organizations. Certainly, the charitable sector has not been immune from episodes of fraud. The Internet as a medium is tailor-made for the purposes of the unscrupulous, requiring little investment to create a flashy Web site that is accessible to tens of millions of potential donors. It may tell about an organization worthy of visitors' donations that may, in fact, consist entirely of a modem, server, HTML file, and the active imagination of an amoral predator.

As almost all of the 1.1 million plus 501(c)s power up their Web sites, (and millions more non-exempt organizations whose requests for donations fall under state solicitation laws), the states would be overwhelmed by a policy of strict enforcement.

And charities face a dilemma as well. From the point of view of a small, locally based charity without the resources to comply with every state law, does it risk being sued by a foreign state simply because it places a general charitable donation request on its Web site? Almost every state that regulates solicitation has an annual filing fee, so it is not just a matter of time and trouble, but a substantial expense as well to register in every state. In my book *The Nonprofit Handbook* (Second Edition), I review the charitable solicitation laws in every state and the District of Columbia. The cost of filing registration statements to comply with all state laws would be at least $1,100 in direct fees for even the smallest charities, and some state fees are scaled to the amount of contributions received. The total could easily reach a few thousand dollars.

The National Association of Attorneys General and the National Association of State Charity Officials met in 1999 to consider, among other issues, how to appropriately regulate charitable solicitation conducted over the Internet. No resolution to this issue was reached at the conference, but participants returned to their states to seek input and study alternative regulatory schemes.

Several suggestions for dealing with this issue have been advanced, some of which received serious consideration at the conference. One possibility is for state regulators to require registration only if the charity targets residents of a foreign state for solicitation, rather than simply placing a passive solicitation request on its Web site. Another option is for a centralized, standardized reporting system to be in place, so that charities that solicit donations on the Internet need only file with a single regulator, with the information available to "consumers" via the Internet. A third possibility is for state law to provide an exemption, at least for small charities, for donations solicited on the Internet.

Even if no changes are made to current state laws, and a small charity is sued by a state regulator for violating a registration law as a result of a Web-based solicitation, it is quite possible that the charity would have a legal defense. In a series of three court cases involving state charitable solicitation laws, the U.S. Supreme Court has overturned state charitable solicitation laws in Maryland and North Carolina. The Court has ruled that these laws placed too heavy a burden on small charities, and thus violated their First Amendment rights of free speech. For a more detailed description of this issue and these cases, visit the Web site:

http://www.muridae.com/nporegulation/documents/
internet_solicitation_law.html

Even if Internet solicitation becomes protected through one strategy or another, charities are not out of the woods. The reason is that it is not likely that a charity that receives an "unsolicited" out-of-state contribution emanating from its Web site will avoid follow-up solicitations, either by mail, telephone, e-mail, or other direct communication.

IRS Substantiation Rules

The federal *Omnibus Budget Reconciliation Act* (OBRA), enacted in 1993, imposed requirements on charities and donors with respect to substantiation of donations for contributions made beginning with the 1994 tax year. The law requires charities to provide a contemporaneous written acknowledgment of contributions of $250 or more when requested by a donor; the donor may not take a charitable tax deduction without having such a written acknowledgment. The practical effect is that charities are sending these statements routinely to their donors as a part of the "thank you" letter. The written acknowledgment must include the amount of cash paid or a description of property transferred by the donor, a statement of whether the donor received goods or services in exchange for the donation, and a good-faith estimate of the value of such goods and services, if any.

The law requires charities that provide goods or services in exchange for the donation, if the donation is in excess of $75, to provide in writing a statement to the donor that the deductibility of the donation is limited to the excess of the amount donated over and above the value of the goods and services provided, and an estimate of the value of those goods and services that were provided by the charity. For example, if your 501(c)(3) organization holds a fundraising dinner and you estimate that your cost of catering and entertainment is $45 per person and you charge $100 per ticket, you must disclose to ticket holders that they can deduct the contribution of $55 per ticket purchased. IRS Revenue Ruling 67-246, 1967-2 C.B. 104 provides examples of fact situations that require this disclosure.

December 1996 final draft regulations issued by the IRS provide some guidance to charities on several issues. First, charities may ignore benefits provided to members that can be used "frequently," such as gift shop discounts, free or discounted parking, or free or discounted admission to the organization's facilities or events. Second, free admission to members-only events can also be ignored if the cost per person does not exceed $6.90. For those who pay more than $75 for a membership package that offers more benefits than a membership at $75 or less, then only the benefits offered to those with membership costs of $75 or less can be ignored when taking the charitable deduction. If an organization offers free admission to a fixed number of events in exchange for membership, then the IRS's interpretation is that the fair market value of the admissions must be deducted from the value of the contribution.

Charities must provide written substantiation of a donation to volunteers who wish to claim as a deduction the cost of unreimbursed expenses of $250 or more. The regulations also require that institutions such as colleges that raise money by offering their alumni the right to purchase hard-to-get athletic tickets must consider 20% of the payment for the tickets as the fair market value for the right to purchase the tickets. No charitable deduction is allowed.

There are many gray areas with respect to substantiation issues, and the IRS has not been totally clear in providing guidance to charities. It makes sense to consult an attorney familiar with this issue if there is any question about whether your organization is in compliance with IRS requirements, particularly if you are selling tickets, conducting auctions, or participating in other e-commerce activities on your Web site that raise legal and tax questions.

Indirect Fundraising

One creative way charities have used the Internet is to place a "wish list" of goods (such as computers, file cabinets and other office equipment, and even vehicles) on their Web sites, and encourage donors to meet those needs by providing either the good or the funds to buy it.

Up Close:

Jason DeVries—Director of Nonprofit Outreach, Shop2Give.com

Jason began his career in the nonprofit sector during college at UCLA, where he worked as a fundraiser for the university, raising money for the Annual Fund, the law school, medical center, and several other programs of the institution. As a political theory major, his senior project was on the topic of Cause-Related Marketing and the Internet. After college, he worked briefly for a national advertising firm as a media buyer, but found the job to be "soul-less and devoid of any significant meaning." Looking for a career that would more directly benefit society, he applied with Shop2Give.com.

"Shop2Give provides an e-commerce solution to charities that allows them to retain a percentage of their constituents' purchases at over 100 Internet merchant sites," he describes. "Building on what we've learned over the past year and a half, we have also begun doing Web design and projects for individual nonprofit organizations. What I do specifically is provide guidance and assistance to clients and prospective clients in all-things-technology. I often find myself designing logos, framing e-mail messages, giving advice about Internet marketing, and answering all sorts of questions. The best part of my job is that I get the chance to help the people that are helping the people."

How is Shop2Give different from the two dozen or so shop-for-charity sites available to consumers?

"First, we were the first charity shopping portal that gave a percentage of purchases to any nonprofit in the United States, allowing consumers a choice of more than 640,000 charities," he notes. "Second, our tracking system is the best in the industry, allowing both the nonprofits and the user to view purchases, click-throughs, and contributions in real time.

"Third, we were the first company to offer the Customized Shopping Mall to nonprofit organizations, which gives each organization its own Web mall page and unique address. And fourth, we do not require registration to Shop2Give. We want people to be able to Shop2Give without being forced to join or divulge information about themselves."

What advice does he offer to nonprofit executives who want to get started in utilizing the Internet and all it has to offer for generating donations and sales of products to benefit their organizations? He offers a four-step strategy.

"The first step, and perhaps most valuable, is to collect e-mail addresses," he recommends. "You would be surprised how few organizations are attempting to do this. Even big organizations have yet to add e-mail to their pledge cards. What a waste.

"The second step is to evaluate your message and how it would best fit online," he suggests. "You might try bringing in some college students for

Excerpt from the Shop2Give home page at http://www.shop2give.com. Reprinted with permission.

a brainstorming session, feed them some pizza, and listen as creative ideas are generated.

"The third step is to build and host your site. Find people you trust that will be available to you at a moment's notice. Depending on the size and budget of your organization, you may want to spend some money to make it look sharp and professionally-designed.

"The fourth step is to develop an e-commerce strategy. There are a couple of different directions you can go here. Shop2Give is one of them. The key to e-commerce is understanding that there are people out there willing to use their expertise to help you establish win-win situations," he contends. "We can't be doing all of this great stuff for free, but if you can show us how we can benefit while you benefit, we will bend over backwards to help. This is true of anyone in this space. The message I would like to pass along as advice is to simply allow tech-savvy people to help you. Tell them what your needs are and see what they say. Bounce ideas off of them and you just might get somewhere with it."

Jason is optimistic that the Internet will eventually become the donation medium of choice.

"I think the sky is the limit with e-philanthropy," he predicts. " I still believe that donors need to be approached in traditional ways to give or to give more, but the Internet certainly could be the transaction at the end of that process. In five years, when we are all wired from rise and shine to beddy-bye, the work done now will pay off for many of these charities that are going out on a limb and adopting new technologies And administratively, using the Internet for fundraising sure beats the pledge card!"

Jason provides seven reasons why the Internet is an attractive fundraising medium compared to conventional methods.

"First, you have a captive audience. When you are on someone's desktop, chances are they chose for you to be there and you have their full attention in a way that was unattainable before. Second, your Web audience is demographically more attractive than the general population qualified audience—computer users have a tendency to have a bit more money per capita. Third, you have the opportunity to reinforce your current message. The Internet gives you a chance to re-present your fundraising appeal to a potential prospect.

"Fourth, your Web site is prospecting for donations while you sleep. You never know when you'll catch someone's interest, and it may well be that Web surfing as a result of a bout of insomnia led to a donation for your organization, directly or indirectly. Fifth, a Web site comes with very little overhead, reducing transaction costs, bureaucracy, administrative time, and, potentially, saving your organization a lot of marketing cost per donor reached. Sixth, with broadband Internet access becoming cheaper and more accessible, charities will have access to high-quality multimedia to convey their message to the masses, for less money than direct mail. And seventh, targeted e-mail is more likely to be much more cost-effective than direct snail mail."

Chapter 6

Online Shopping Malls

Introduction

Just imagine. Instead of going to their favorite mall to make a purchase of a national brand product, your charity's friends and supporters go online and visit a Web site that charges them the customary (and often discounted) price, and funnels a percentage of the purchase price directly to your charity. Their purchases from retailers and discounters such as Toys R Us, Amazon.com, and Sharper Image are delivered on their doorstep within a day or two, and your charity receives a check aggregating all of these donations, no strings attached.

This is not the future.

This scenario is occurring thousands of times each day on scores of Web sites, and the number of such transactions is expanding exponentially. Online retailing accounted for just .5% of purchases made in 1998, but climbed to 1.2% in 1999 (to an estimated $38-40 billion), according to one report. Intense competition is just beginning among for-profit entrepreneurs to obtain the cooperation of charities in directing traffic to their sites. I think that this new development is very positive for both charities and consumers, although both need to be aware of limitations and potential problems associated with this trend.

Many in the charitable community have had a love-hate relationship with the private sector. We benefit from the generosity of grants and donations from capitalist enterprises, while at the same time we denigrate the exploitation and lack of altruism inherent in rampant commercialism and consumerism. After all, many charities (and government programs, as well) were initiated because of the failure of the market to address many human needs.

Some of the entrepreneurs who have initiated these collaborative programs with charities have a genuine desire to parlay their commercial success into socially responsible activities that benefit society. And others, no doubt, cynically recognize that they can generate revenue by serving as middlemen and reaching a new market of consumers attracted by the incentive of helping their favorite charity. Regardless of the reasons motivating these startup "dot-com" companies, the advent of e-commerce has seen a proliferation of for-profit Web sites geared to combine the joys of shopping with the imperative of helping the less fortunate. They are likely here to stay.

Among the more-prominent charity-shopper sites are (in alphabetical order):

> 4charity.com *(http://www.4charity.com)*
> Charitycounts.com *(http://www.charitycounts.com)*
> Charitymall.com *(http://www.charitymall.com)*
> GreaterGood.com *(http://www.greatergood.com)*
> iGive.com *(http://www.igive.com)*
> ihelpsupport.com *(http://www.ihelpsupport.com)*
> ireachout.com *(http://www.ireachout.com)*
> Nonprofit Shopping Mall (http://www.npsmall.com)
> Shop2Bless *(http://www.shop2bless.com)*
> Shop2Give *(http://www.shop2give.com)*
> Shop4Change.com *(http://www.shop4change.com)*
> ShopGenerocity.com *(http://www.shopgenerocity.com)*

The legitimacy and appropriateness of the marriage between charities and for-profit online shopping malls was the subject of stimulating debate on electronic mailing lists during late 1999 and early 2000. With few exceptions, most participants in this debate from the charitable sector, including those who work for charities that have signed up with these malls, are satisfied with these arrangements. Donations, that, to this point, have generally been meager, are not the only benefit. Those who work for charities also see the benefit of promoting the work of their organizations—some of these shopper Web sites include areas that provide information about participating charities. Criticisms from the charities about these arrangements, while muted to this point, focus on a few issues. Some charitable executives fear that if the public becomes comfortable with supporting charities by shopping, they won't continue supporting them with conventional donations. Others are concerned about the long-term financial viability of the site sponsors and the continued willingness of the merchants to provide rebates in the face of mounting competition for the retail dollar. Few startup dot-com companies are making a profit, and those in the industry recognize that there is a need to make substantial investments today without the expectation of profits many years down the road. Only a few are likely to be eventually profitable, and many are likely to disappear in a year or two.

The legal issues that arise as a result of these partnerships are unexplored territory, and there may be some gray areas worthy of discussion. First, it is not entirely clear that the value of donations made through purchases is tax-deductible, as is claimed by some of these sites. Second, if purchases are made directly from a charity's Web site, it is possible that the charity may be subject to unrelated business income taxes (as one might expect, considering the past egregious misinterpretations by the IRS of UBIT laws). Third, if a charity promotes the commercial site in its newsletters and other mailings, it may put its preferential postal rates at risk.

Tips

For those who are considering participating in one of these partnerships, I offer the following advice:

1. Ask lots of questions. Know exactly what your commitments and responsibilities are with respect to the agreement or contract. Direct your questions not only to the shopping mall staff, but to charities that are already participating.

2. Don't commit your organization to pay anything for participating. Most legitimate shopper partnerships do not charge anything to the charity. You may have to expend some resources to upgrade your organization's Web site to accommodate the agreement and send out promotional materials, but there should be no upfront fees involved to participate.

3. Review the Web site of the sponsor from top to bottom. Read the site's FAQ (most legitimate sites have one). Read and feel comfortable with the privacy policy (most legitimate sites have one). Make sure you are comfortable with the merchant list.

4. Don't agree to an exclusivity provision that would prohibit your organization from signing up with another shopping mall Web site. There is no benefit to you from an exclusive contract, and with the intense competition going on, you may get a better deal from a site tomorrow that might not even exist today.

5. Understand how and when your organization will receive checks. Is it monthly or quarterly? Does there need to be a minimum amount for you to receive a donation? What is the lag time between a purchase and the receipt by your organization of the donation? All of these vary with the sponsor.

6. Know what the sponsor expects from your charity. Do they want you to provide them with the e-mail addresses of everyone on your board and membership so they can target unsolicited and annoying promotional messages to your constituency? Just say no.

7. Make sure that the level to which you promote commercial activities in your newsletters and other mailings will not disqualify you from nonprofit mailing status.

8. Verify that the sponsor provides adequate customer service. You want to make sure that purchasers with a problem will be complaining to them about problems that may crop up, rather than to your organization. Some services have their own customer service departments, while others depend on the retailers. Obviously, the former policy is an advantage to your organization.

9. Know what your organization's commitment will be with respect to ending the relationship, in the event that this becomes necessary for any reason.

10. Consider the track record/trust factor in your decision. Are you comfortable with the motivations of the founders? Are their members and merchants growing? Are there any records of complaints against them filed with the Better Business Bureau? Are they comfortable answering your questions, or do they make you feel that you are a nuisance wasting their time?

11. Consider who in your organization will authorize the decision on participation. Can it be made by the executive director alone, the executive director in consultation with the board chair, or does a decision need to be made by the board?

Up Close: ## Randi Shade, Co-founder Charitygift.com

Hundreds, if not thousands, of dot-com startups launched in 1999 and 2000 while this book was being written, many of them involving some aspect of interest to philanthropy. A staff member of one of these new startups contacted me by e-mail in January 2000 to comment on a book I co-wrote with Gary Grant, the *Nonprofit Internet Handbook.* He told me about the startup he was involved with, and requested that I check it out. I did so, and exchanged some e-mailed comments with Randi Shade, the co-founder of this startup that permits members of the public to send customized greeting cards to people, include a donation to any one of 680,000 charities, and pay for it by credit card. The service sends the card to the recipient, sends the donation to the charity, and charges $4.95-$6.95 for the card (depending on the quantity ordered) plus the credit card transaction fee of 3%. The purchaser designs the card online from templates.

It wasn't until five months later that I experienced the death of a close friend and colleague who was active in several local charities. Rather than go to a store and purchase a card and send a separate communication with a donation to her favorite charity, I decided to try out Charitygift.com. I was pleasantly surprised by the convenience and the site's creativity in allowing me to personalize my message to the family of the deceased. Everything I needed was accomplished with a few clicks of the mouse and my MasterCard.

Charities are benefiting from new business models. This is one example. The following, reprinted with permission, is an excerpt of the e-mail message I received from Ms. Shade describing her experience in the startup of this Texas-based dot-com.

"My partners and I launched Charitygift specifically to meet unmet customer needs. We get paid by customers willing to pay for the products and services we sell, but that only happens if we meet their needs. I realize it is a strange notion in all the dot-com madness, (and you're right it costs a fortune to get the word out about our product—a fortune we don't have right now), but it is our hope that we will eventually sell enough of our products and services to one day be a profitable company.

"Earlier this year when a friend of mine passed away, the obituary said 'in lieu of flowers, please make a contribution to ....' Three charities were listed; my friend had volunteered at each of them. By the time I looked up the address of one of the organizations, wrote and mailed a check, bought and mailed a condolence card to my friend's family, and called the charity to ask for a tax receipt, I had spent a lot of time and several dollars on cards, postage and telephone calls. The organization added me to its mailing list, still hasn't sent an acknowledgment to my friend's family as far as I know, and yet it is one of the best AIDS hospices in the country. I wanted to send a meaningful gift to the family of my friend to let them know how much their son meant to me. I was happy to help an organization that meant so much to my friend even if it was one I had never heard of before, and I am glad to have learned the organization does good work even if it isn't very good at handling administrative things.

"Charitygift is a response to this. It is also a response to all the useless gifts exchanged by people every year. We founded Charitygift to create a gift product that is as easy to send as flowers, but that benefits charity rather than dying in a vase a few days later or gathering dust on a shelf. I worked throughout much of my career as a nonprofit fundraising professional, most recently as the Director of Development for a Boston-based national nonprofit called City Year. My convictions about certain things were very strong as a result. I believed it was important to create something new—to increase the total charitable giving pie, not just redistribute costs associated with fundraising. Most of our corporate customers this holiday season would have sent pens, popcorn tins, or cookies. By using Charitygift, money went to charity that would have otherwise gone to retailers selling seemingly useless gifts If just one percent of the gift-giving dollars were spent exchanging Charitygift cards instead of other things, it would mean literally hundreds of millions of new dollars for charity.

"A second aspect to this thought was that I wanted to be sure Charitygift truly made its money by selling valuable products and services that are above and beyond the charitable donation. One-hundred percent of every Charitygift donation goes to charity for that reason. Any charity can benefit from Charitygift donations and there are no strings attached. Other for-profit companies in the online charity space seem to be merely acting as third-party, commission-driven professional fundraising services; being online and having a dot-com at the end of the name doesn't make it any more original. That said, some could prove to be quite profitable some day. But, we wanted Charitygift to be unique; we didn't want it to be an online version of the same old thing.

"We knew we had a great idea because we knew too many people, including ourselves, who would buy a Charitygift if it was available. We conducted market research anyway to convince a few investors and to give us an even better understanding of our potential customers. We held focus groups and did an online consumer survey to test our business concept. We used a sample size of 1,000 respondents. These respondents were pre-screened to ensure we had demographic, geographic, socioeconomic, and gender diversity in our sample consistent with the population of America. Across the board, we found a majority of people willing to buy our product if we made it available. There was very little price sensitivity, and people viewed the key benefits of the concept to be its uniqueness, its convenience, and that it demonstrates caring. We considered all that, and then we got busy. Generosity in a to-go box was born."

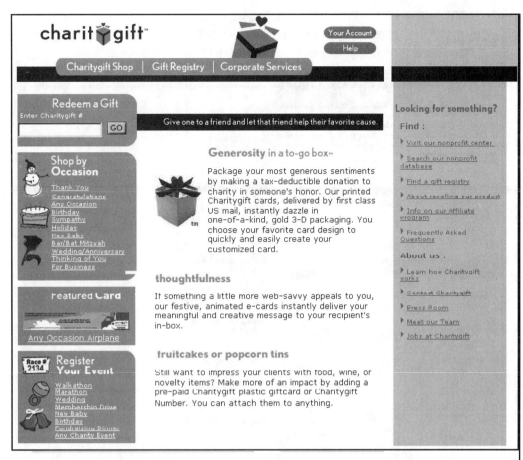

An excerpt from the Charitygift home page at http://www.charitygift.com.
Reprinted with permission.

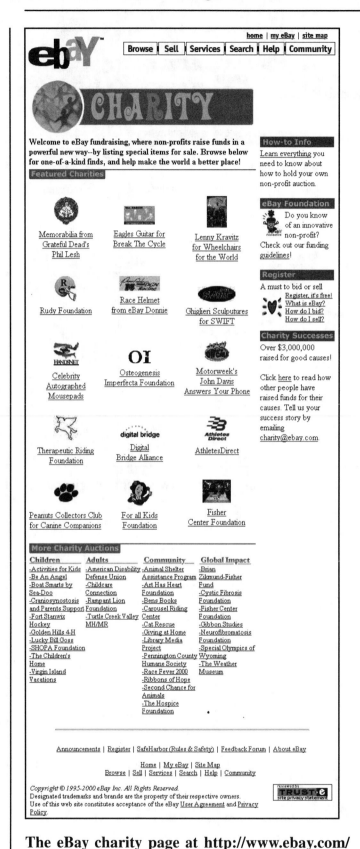

The eBay charity page at http://www.ebay.com/ charity. These materials have been reproduced by White Hat Communications with the permission of eBay, Inc. Copyright © EBAY, Inc. All rights reserved.

Chapter 7

Charity Auctions

Introduction

Going once, going twice, gone! Because of the versatility of the Internet, traditional methods of fundraising may soon become an anachronism. Fundraising executives are reevaluating their techniques and strategies for generating revenues for their organizations, and innovative uses of the Internet are cropping up in news reports. The online charity auction is one such innovation.

According to a study released this year by Jupiter Communications (http://www.jup.com), the online auction industry will generate $3.2 billion annually by 2002 with total spending at online auctions over the next four years of $7.1 billion. Furthermore, the number of participants in these auctions will explode from 1.2 million in 1998 to 6.5 million in 2002. Of those who shop online, fully 11 percent participate in online auctions.

Online charity auctions is one new business model that is being almost universally lauded by those who try it.

Success Stories

Last year, the American Red Cross recorded millions of dollars in supplemental contributions for its Kosovo refugee relief effort by participating in charity auctions hosted by some of the best-known online retailers with auction facilities, including eBay, Amazon.com, Yahoo!, Livebid.com, and Up4sale.com.

Other online charity auction success stories have made headlines. A year ago, rock star Eric Clapton auctioned off 100 guitars and raised $5 million for the drug treatment clinic he founded.

E-Trade Canada hosted an online auction that raised funds for the Canadian Foundation for AIDS Research. The American Cancer Society, with the sponsorship of Amazon.com and Harley Davidson, raised funds with an online auction of celebrity-autographed memorabilia.

An X-Files online fan club raised more than $100,000 last year for charity. Another fan club, the official Gillian Anderson Web site (GAWS) [http://gaws.ao.net] scheduled it fourth annual online auction in May 2000. Its previous auctions raised $6,000, $23,000, and $90,000 respectively. All proceeds benefit Anderson's favorite charity, Neurofibromatosis, Inc.

HandsNet (see page 156) raised more than $5,000 by conducting celebrity auctions on eBay, more than $1,500 in the first month of participation. Items that were auctioned were mousepads signed by Mr. Rogers, Regis Philbin, and Jesse Ventura. Others who have donated items for this auction were Jane Fonda and Oprah Winfrey. (For the full story on this and other successes, visit eBay's auction site at http://www.eBay.com/charity.) The auctions not only raised funds for HandsNet's scholarship program, but also promoted the organization to hundreds of eBay viewers who might never have heard of the organization, according to an interview with HandsNet's Director of Online Community Development, Ken Goldstein, that was posted on eBay's Web site.

Advantages Compared to Conventional Auctions

Online auctions have a number of advantages over conventional ones.

- You can auction off an almost infinite number of items.
- The auction can last for hours or months.
- Everyone can participate, even if they would not have found the time convenient for a conventional auction.
- People can participate from all over the world.
- The design and administration of the online auction can be performed online, providing home-bound volunteers, or those busy during traditional business or meeting hours, with an opportunity to volunteer their services.
- Turnkey operations (see below) abound to assist you in startup.

Scores of "dot-com" for-profit companies are competing for the right to host charitable auctions, and many provide these services free-of-charge to charities. As with online shopping partnerships described in the previous chapter, there are unique aspects of each for-profit host, and charities should be choosy and informed about the advantages and disadvantages of each. Some hosts, such as Yahoo!, provide their "backoffice" services transparently, so that donors can visit the charity's Web site and access all the information they need to participate. This requires the charity to actively generate traffic to its auction site, arrange item categories, and make sure the items auctioned get sent to the winning bidder. Other hosts can provide a soup-to-nuts menu of services, but generate Web hits for the commercial partner (and its advertisers) rather than the charity.

What does it cost? With a bit of ingenuity, a charity auction can be administered using eBay for a modest few dollars. Or you can buy a Cadillac by having Ten97.com put together your entire event, including promotion, and even provide items to supplement your celebrity auction catalog, for fees ranging "from $7,500 to $435,000, depending upon the size and scope of TEN97's fund-raising events and promotional services."

The point here is that you can pay a little or a lot.

Among some of the charity auction sites that have been publicizing their services are (in alphabetical order):

4Charity.com—*http://www.4charity.com*
Amazon.com—*http://www.livebid.amazon.com*
Causelink—*http://www.causelink.com*
CBid—*http://www.cbid.com*
Charitableway—*http://www.Charitableway.com*
CharityCounts—*http://www.charitycounts.com*
CommunityBids—*http://www.communitybids.com*
DonationMarketplace—*http://www.Donationmarketplace.com*
DonorNet—*http://www.donornet.com*
eBay—*http://www.ebay.com*
FundraisingAuctions—*http:/www.fundraisingauctions.com*
iCharity—*http://www.icharity.net*
Membership4U—*http://www.membership4u.com*
SoldAbsolute—*http://www.Soldabsolute.com*
Ten97—*http://www.Ten97.com*
Up4Sale—*http://www.up4sale.com*
WebCharity—*http://www.webcharity.com*
Yahoo!—*http://www.yahoo.com*
Yardsale—*http://www.yardsale-net.com*

Tips

Here are some of my suggestions for running an online charity auction through a commercial provider, some of which are identical to those for online shopping agreements:

1. If you have the expertise, keep the portal for your organization's charity auction on your own Web site—creating an online community and keeping hits from potential donors on your site, not that of a commercial provider.

2. Scan pictures of the items you have for auction and post them online.

3. Don't restrict publicity of your auction to online Web site notices, electronic mailing lists, and e-mail. Use PSAs, newsletters, your local newspapers, snail mail postcards, and conventional publicity flyers.

4. Send e-mail thank yous to successful bidders. Mail out the items to successful bidders promptly, along with the required substantiation letter.

5. If you are contracting out your charity auction to an online commercial service, ask lots of questions. Know exactly what your commitments and responsibilities are with respect to the agreement or contract. Direct your questions not only to the auction staff, but to other charities that have participated with that commercial host.

6. Don't commit your organization to pay anything for participating unless you are sure that such payments are appropriate and reasonable. Many host companies do not charge anything to the charity. You will have to expend some resources to change your organization's Web site to accommodate the auction and send out promotional materials. If upfront fees are charged, make sure these services are not typically provided free.

7. Review the Web site of the sponsor from top to bottom. Read the site's FAQ (most legitimate sites have one). Read and feel comfortable with the privacy policy (most legitimate sites have one).

8. Understand how and when your organization will receive its payments from successful bidders.

9. Know what the sponsor expects from your charity. Do they want you to provide them with the e-mail addresses of everyone on your board and membership so they can target unsolicited and annoying promotional messages to your constituency? Just say no.

10. Know what your organization's commitment will be with respect to ending the relationship, in the event that this becomes necessary for any reason.

11. Consider the track record/trust factor in your decision. Are you comfortable with the motivations of the founders? Are there any records of complaints against them filed with the Better Business Bureau? Are they comfortable answering your questions, or do they make you feel that you are a nuisance wasting their time?

    For charities, the online charitable auction model is becoming another arrow in the quiver for creative strategies to generate online donations and other revenue.

Up Close:

Gary Grant—Director of Major Gifts, University of Chicago Medical Center

Gary Grant has a long association with both fundraising and the Internet, and his expertise in both areas plays a major role in the success he has as the Director of Major Gifts for the University of Chicago Medical Center.

His development career began as an undergraduate student volunteer telephone solicitor, and he estimates that he raised more than $1 million through chatting over the phone with alumni over a two-year period. What he enjoyed most was sharing his academic experience and hearing about the experiences of his alumni prospects. The telephone interaction strengthened relationships, and Gary feels that this bond inevitably increased the number of, and amount of, contributions—an observation that he has incorporated into his online activities.

After graduation, Gary took a job as an Assistant Director of Development, running the college's fifth reunion fundraising program and annual gifts for Chicago and Detroit. He also directed the institution's Parents Fund. From there, he served three years as Associate Director of the Social Work graduate school. Law school beckoned and after graduating from ITT Chicago-Kent College of Law, he returned to the social work school as an Associate Dean, in charge of both development and alumni/public relations.

"Soon after I began, in 1994, the Internet was just becoming part of the mainstream," he remembers. "Maybe 25% of the graduate-level social work schools even had a Web page. When a student asked the Dean why our school did not have one, she said that he should build one for us. He did, but when he graduated, I volunteered to maintain it. Over time, I self-taught myself how to write HTML, so I could begin to use this page for certain activities that would promote the school and increase interaction with our graduates and others."

Did he run into any political problems in trying to get a consensus about various aspects of the institution's site, such as the level of privacy, security, or content?

"Absolutely!" he reports. "Trying to make everyone happy with its design is a challenge. I've been fortunate that I've had full control over sites I've maintained, so no one else could battle too much about my design choices and rationale. Within the institution, there was oftentimes some resistance to innovation online, for example, putting names of students on the site." The fear was that putting student names online would result in harassment from crackpots or spamming messages to students. Fortunately, he says, students did not blame the institution when the rare instance of misuse did occur, and they were quite grateful for the convenience it provided them in communicating with one another.

Despite skepticism from some of his colleagues who felt that the Web was a fad and a waste of time and resources, Gary believed that this new medium held tremendous potential, especially for drawing the institution's constituency into a closer and more interactive relationship, and would eventually become a key strategy for institutional advancement. He remains proud of his Web site innovations, such as developing a mentor page, a historical photo archive, and an online student journal. He also started using the Internet to organize online events, and found the benefits positive.

"Rural alumni we could never visit were not only hearing from us, but interacting. It created a bridge between alumni long gone and the students now there...and in so doing bridged our funding constituency to our mission," he says.

"On an individual level, we were also using the Internet to bring our donors closer," he points out. "Although it took some time to become more confident in e-mailing individuals who were significant actual or potential funders, it quickly became the favored method of communication for some and allowed them to have the closer connection with the school that makes philanthropy much more likely."

Gary finds that a professional Web site with content useful to potential donors likely creates positive relationships that enhance fundraising opportunities.

"I recently worked with an individual seeking to fund a new Center for the study of a specific disease that, though little is understood about it, affects many people," Gary points out as an example. "The donor made it clear that the creation of a Web presence in order to expand awareness was essential. My experience is helping me to shape this into something that will fill a unique niche in this area without being duplicative of existing resources. Without a clear and sensible Internet strategy, this donor very easily might have been less satisfied or encouraged about making his gift."

He sees that this model is generally applicable to the nonprofit sector.

"Most nonprofits have a lot of information they would like to disseminate publicly, and what better way than to—at virtually no cost—publish globally," he observes.

"Millions are starting to understand the Internet as a source for community and interaction. When they go online, it's not always to read an article, press release, or guidebook. Many want another human being to be there and to have the relatively immediate satisfaction of just simply connecting. It is there that the development profession has its biggest opportunity," he continues. "Reading about how wonderful your nonprofit is may not encourage gifts. Finding the answer to a question may not motivate the gift. But connecting to your mission online can make a big difference."

So, what should be the strategy of using the Internet for fundraising? Gary offers this three-part advice:

"First, you must build an online audience that has a sense of member- ship. Second, once recruited, online members will need to be given satis- fying opportunities to interact with the agency and/or its mission directly. And third, based on the strength of this connection, solicitations may perhaps be made online," he advises.

Gary also offers advice for those nonprofit staff who are contemplating making a major investment into the new e-commerce technologies.

"My main advice would be to consider all the ideas others implement, but to understand that there is not one right model here. The most important thing to do is to concentrate on what is your mission, who is the constitu- ency you serve, and who are the people who support now or might support your organization," he says. "Then you can develop some creative possi- bilities for interacting—considering ways to get people to your site and make sure they are delighted by the experience."

Gary is a firm believer that quality is more important than quantity with respect to the "hits" the site receives. "Remember that having a hundred people who are uniquely delighted to visit your site and who feel con- nected and involved as a result is probably better than a thousand who simply skim through," he concludes.

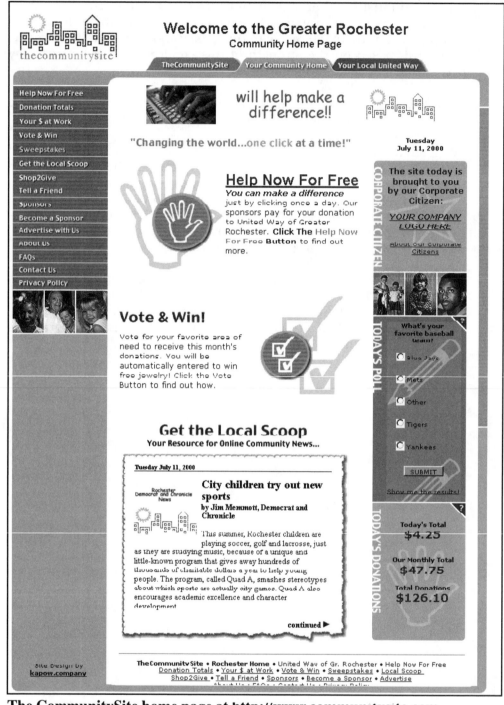

The CommunitySite home page at http://www.communitysite.com.
Reprinted with permission.

Chapter 8

Online Communities

Introduction

It is not likely that your organization will be able to compete with America Online and attract 20 plus million members who will spend hours and hours each week visiting your site. But the AOL product, and that of some of the most familiar names on the Internet, from eBay to Yahoo!, to Lycos, to HandsNet, have made their mark by creating and maintaining online communities of loyal Web site visitors. Loyal visitors build relationships. Whether it is through donations, opportunities to volunteer or participate in advocacy efforts, product purchases, or simply feedback, nonprofit organizations thrive on relationships with individuals. There is perhaps no better strategy to build relationships on the Internet than establishing an online community.

What is an Online Community?

An online community is an integrated set of services that is available at a single Web site, attracting people who have something in common. The types of services that are typically available are real time chat, forums or message boards, member directories, instant messaging (such as AOL's "buddy" program), job/career information, shopping, and news and information. What members of the site have in common may be their age, their social status, their profession, their religion, their politics, some health concern, or interest in a particular public policy issue.

What distinguishes online communities from other Web sites is that much of the content is contributed by visitors with something in common.

Examples of Online Communities

Just this year, I have participated in three nonprofit-related online communities. Unlike AOL, which charges about $20/month for access to a wide range of Internet services and extensive content, most are free. Typically, I would receive an e-mail, postcard, or other notice (such as in the organizational newsletter) informing me that a new online community is being established and inviting my participation. There may be some hook that encourages me to join, either offering some service I might need (such as permanent e-mail or a directory of some sort) or a discount on merchandise. In the case of the first one I joined, DraGoNet, I was attracted by the search engine that permitted me to look up former classmates, even if all I had was their first name and year of graduation.

DraGoNet (www.DraGoNet.org) is hosted by the Drexel University Alumni Association. On this site, one can have access to chat rooms, forums, career information, a student directory, free permanent e-mail, and, of course, shopping for Drexel-related and other merchandise.

A second online community that I joined was ASPANet, the Web site of the American Society for Public Administration (ASPA). This is a professional membership organization, and registration in the online community is free, but restricted to association members. Among the services provided are free personal Web site hosting, permanent e-mail, career services, and message boards.

The third online community, Jenzabar, is a for-profit site that partners with college professors (see below).

E-Commerce and Online Communities

Online communities and e-commerce create a natural marriage. Visitors to online communities tend to be loyal, returning again and again, often night after night. What attracts them is the opportunity to interact with people like themselves. The experience is enhanced when technology permits this interaction to occur in real time. Today, a visitor comes to the site and may linger, look around the site, and discover products and services for sale that are tailored for a particular niche market.

Tomorrow (and that day may be this year or next), these visitors may be clicking on a product and have the ability to talk to each other in real time to compare notes, discuss their preferences, and do in virtual reality what shoppers do in real shopping malls. Research has shown that shoppers like to communicate while they are shopping online, and technology is coming to facilitate this. Amazon.com has taken advantage of this fact by providing electronic feedback that is available to shoppers. A prospective book buyer can see reviews posted by those who recently purchased the book, and they can see a list of other books that were purchased by those who also bought a book of interest. Amazon.com encourages members of the reading public to submit reviews, which are posted online on the same page as the book being sold.

Online communities support business transactions by helping to drive targeted traffic to your site. Once they are there, it is up to you to find ways to keep them there.

How to Create an Online Community

Those online communities that are successful are the ones that have found a way to reach a critical mass of participants. I took a graduate school class recently, and my professor required everyone in the class to join an online community, Jenzabar.com. The intent was to distribute class assignments, enhance communication among the members of the class through class-specific online forums, and build a community among the class members. The platform provided by Jenzabar.com, a for-profit company, was a first-class effort. The tools were there. However, the members of the class never became comfortable with this online community. Feeling frustrated, I agreed to seed messages in the forums and try to generate some controversy and passion. It just never worked; the response was lukewarm. Other classes, however, reported a much more positive experience.

I noticed a similar problem with Microsoft Network's nonprofit forums when I was reviewing this site for the 1998 book, *The Nonprofit Internet Handbook*. Again, the platform was first class. But virtually all of the messages came from one person, who obviously was handpicked by Microsoft to generate content.

I recommend that you find at least a dozen people who are committed to the online community concept, and have them all agree to actively participate. Obviously, no one will come back to a chat room that doesn't have anyone in it, or has people making small talk. Publicity must be focused and fierce! People will need a good reason to visit and register. Make it worth their while. Advertise on electronic mailing lists and in your newsletters. Send e-mail and snail mail to your donors, and make sure all organization staff join and participate.

Linda Grobman, my wife, established an online community for social workers and social work students in 1995 that is still going strong. To meet the unique needs of her community (which also keeps people coming back), she holds periodic, moderated chats on the same evening each week (with a devoted community member volunteering as host), moderates a message board, provides discounts for products in the site's store, and, far and away the most popular feature, posts lots of new job listings. She advertises the site in publications geared to her target market, such as the monthly tabloid of the National Association of Social Workers. But the primary source of the site's continued growth is her own active participation in the social work community-at-large—both online and off-line.

Challenges of Online Communities

1. Creating and maintaining an online community requires substantial time and effort.

2. Some visitors inappropriately post, such as putting slanderous or libelous messages on the message board, posting commercial messages, violating confidentiality, or infringing on a copyright.

3. Some words used in real time posting may be offensive, requiring the use of filtering software. It is difficult to choose which words to censor.

4. Online communities need an effective Code of Conduct (see Appendix G).

Even when the online community is free, almost every one requires members to register, select a user name, and select a password. Doing so assures that the site has at least a minimum of control over denying access to those who consistently violate its Code of Conduct. There are also marketing reasons to have a password-protected site.

"Passwords and Usernames really aren't a good or bad thing," says Matt Sloan of Silicon Planet (http://www.siliconplanet.com), an online community for fundraisers. "It depends on how each community wants to use it—meaning, how open or exclusive do you want it to be?"

Matt believes that having an exclusive online community can both appeal to or turn off users, depending on who they are.

"Some enjoy the coziness and security of this sort of community, thinking once they log in, they are entering a private area consisting of others like them," he says. "Those who don't like to log in a username and password feel that this is an added hassle of being online (and feel that) the community (should) be open to all and not (be) like a private country club. I've actually heard people describe it as such."

One benefit of these access restrictions is the ability to enforce the rules of the online community.

"I think that if you want to create a viable and responsible community, you need to hold strong to your Code of Conduct," Sloan observes. "I've seen and heard of so many open community/discussion boards where a couple of loose cannons make it an uncomfortable and less inviting place for users to go. Taking away access (from violators) enables online communities to maintain their integrity and interest. By doing this, users feel safe belonging to the community, and thus they'll keep coming back."

Legal Issues

Establishing an online community exposes the organization to legal liability in a number of areas that are unsettled, chiefly because of the fact that many technology issues are new and haven't been tested in the courts. It is not unusual for landmark cases to take 10 years before they are resolved by the U.S. Supreme Court, and commercial use of the Internet is barely that old. In 1996, the Congress enacted *The Communications Decency Act*, which has a provision that under certain conditions, a service provider is not the "publisher" when a user posts material on an interactive Web site that is considered defamatory. This provision was upheld in U.S. District Court in a case decided in 1998 involving America Online and political columnist Matt Drudge.

A Code of Conduct is a necessity (see Appendix G), as is a privacy statement.

The Code should include what behaviors are not permitted by site users, such as flaming; obscene, sexist, anti-Semitic or racist postings; the posting of copyrighted material without permission from the copyright owner; the uploading of files, such as software or other materials that are a violation of intellectual property laws; and engaging in fraudulent conduct or harassment of other users.

One concern pointed out by legal experts is that your Web site is accessible globally, and each country has its own laws with respect to what is acceptable content. It is not clear how the courts will enforce the laws of foreign countries with respect to content on your U.S.-based site.

An excellent summary of the legal issues surrounding online communities is provided by John Delaney, senior co-editor of *Online Community Report* (See: *Online Communities and the Law*, http:/www.OnlineCommunityReport. com/features/law). The Web site for *Online Community Report* (http:// www.onlinecommunityreport.com/ is an indispensable resource for those who run and frequent online communities.

Up Close: Jacqueline Read
Maine Philanthropy Center

Jacqueline serves as the Director for Library and Communications of The Maine Philanthropy Center, a Regional Association of Grantmakers affiliated with the national Forum of Regional Associations of Grantmakers in Washington, D.C. The association provides philanthropic research and educational opportunities to the Third Sector in Maine and partners with other Maine and New England organizations to promote effective philanthropy throughout the region.

Jacqueline teaches two workshops, "Search! Philanthropy on the 'Net" and "E-Philanthropy" for the Center and speaks about the association's work on panels across the state. Currently, her board service includes the Maine Writers & Publishers Alliance and Maine Initiatives, a funder for social change. Jacqueline moved to Maine in 1997 and brought a background as a small business owner in a nationally recognized trade show photography concern to her entrepreneurial take on philanthropy. She has years of experience as a volunteer with nonprofits, and expresses confidence that the nonprofit sector can and will pay attention to, and participate in, e-commerce and e-philanthropy.

"For many, many nonprofits in Maine, e-commerce is a brand new concept," she explains. "We spend our time looking at the possibilities and the providers. I heard one great story here: the town of Mansfield, Maine, held an online auction and raised over $8,000 for its coffers! I like to tell this story because it demonstrates what small towns and small nonprofits can do."

Jacqueline expects that the level of comfort with Internet giving will continue to grow.

"Conventional wisdom has it that a generation raised on the Internet will expect online interaction with nonprofits," she says. "It makes sense that individuals doing their banking and purchasing online will use the option of writing an electronic check to the nonprofits they support. A simple statement in an annual appeal letter along the lines of 'for your convenience, you can send your donation via the Internet at www.xyz.org' will appear first on paper and perhaps later on e-mail solicitations."

 She says the experience of online stock market trading can provide lessons to the voluntary sector as to what pitfalls are involved in e-commerce.

"Investors are demanding that virtual organizations make a profit in the foreseeable future," she says, suggesting as evidence the major "correction" in the NASDAQ that occurred in the spring of 2000. "Even Amazon.com, the darling of Wall Street, is staring down the barrel of disgruntled investors. If a for-profit provider cannot figure out a way to make money from its nonprofit clientele, it will change its business model," she predicts. "Unlike the old name brands like Sears or J.C. Penney, it's increasingly difficult to know which for-profit provider will be in business in the long run. In Internet time, two years is often considered a long time to be in business (not that there's any guarantee for Sears or J.C. Penney anymore!)."

Like many who follow e-philanthropy, Jacqueline marvels at the success of the American Red Cross, but thinks that in time, many other charities will reap major benefits by luring donations over the Internet as a result of relationships begun with to Web page visits.

"Everyone talks about the American Red Cross and its ability to raise some hundreds of thousands of dollars via the Internet during a crisis," she observes. "It showed that people are willing to donate on the 'Net and that this medium is conducive to rapid action. But the American Red Cross is a well-known entity," she notes. "Reports from the field indicate that few nonprofits who are not as well known as the Red Cross are raising big money on the Web —yet. Still, I think the potential is there for Web donations to become another way in which a donor can be supportive. I don't think it will happen with a big marketing 'bang,' but slowly, as nonprofits market their electronic presence and provide e-donation as one of many ways to provide support. Eventually it will reach critical mass and a nonprofit not on the 'Net will be at a distinct disadvantage."

As someone with an organization whose mission is to help Maine charities reach their full potential, Jacqueline shares advice for those who want to get started on developing an e-commerce and e-philanthropy strategy for their organizations.

"There is no lack of information on the Web about e-philanthropy!" she asserts. "I'd suggest the executive start with sites he/she trusts—the National Association of Nonprofit Organizations (http:www.ncna.org), Independent Sector (http://www.independentsector.org), Guidestar (http://www.guidestar.org), and American Association of Fund Raising Counsel site (http://www.oramgroup.com/aafrc.html), For a reasonable overview, Kellogg Foundation released a good, easy-to-understand report in February (note: see page 160). Then, I'd strongly suggest that the executive join an Internet mailing list focusing on online fundraising."

Jacqueline thinks it is entirely possible for charities, even small ones, to avoid the expense of application service providers (ASPs), portal providers, and high-priced Web development consultants and develop a credible e-philanthropy and e-commerce site on their own. But there are advantages as well in seeking outside assistance.

"A simple Web site using a donation mechanism through, as just one example, helping.org is easily doable by most small nonprofits," she judges. "But, when the organization wants to extend its range of services, Application Service Providers are going to be the best bet. They can create economies of scale that a single nonprofit, unless it's one of the very large nonprofit agencies, probably will never be able to afford." She believes that for-profit businesses have taken advantage of ASPs for some time, and that there will always be a market for those vendors who can capture the unique needs of nonprofits at a price they can afford.

However, those who see use of the Internet as simply a cash cow are missing the point, she contends.

"The new technology is not only about fundraising," she argues. "It's also about increased efficiency across the organization. I suspect it's been the idea of raising dollars that has prompted so much interest in the Internet, but in many ways it's a red herring at the present time. Nonprofit organizations should be on the Internet for much more basic reasons: e-mail, the ability to share files across offices, and the ability to communicate with peers nationwide at a fraction of the cost—to use just some examples of how nonprofits should be using the new technology. If it takes e-donation to motivate charity executives to look closely at the 'Net, then so be it. Raising dollars can come from cost-savings just as easily or even more easily than coming from donors."

Does she feel that anything is being lost by conducting our "business" over the Internet rather than F2F?

"That depends on the organization," she maintains. "I personally support two national nonprofits. I've yet to meet anyone from those organizations, but the work they do secures our support on a yearly basis. The Internet has the unique ability to foster communities of like-minded supporters across the nation and around the globe. But for small, local nonprofits, it would be a mistake to only use the Internet. For them, the 'Net will probably remain a way to keep in touch with and offer e-donation to current supporters."

What are her views about the future of e-commerce for nonprofits?

"Clearly, very promising," she says. "I think it will take off more slowly in the nonprofit sector because of the crushing demands already upon agencies. Providers can offer the best and most-sophisticated products in the world, but if the nonprofit organization doesn't have staff or money, it cannot take advantage of them. There are people who say that if nonprofits don't take advantage of emerging technologies right NOW they'll be left behind." This is one opinion, often heard on fundraising electronic mailing lists, that she disputes.

"Behind what?" she asks rhetorically. "Nonprofits have shown more resilience, creativity and determination on fewer dollars than most for-profits can imagine. There is huge heart at work in most of these agencies and while they may pick up on technology at a slower pace, they are in no danger of falling by the wayside. These are the folks who bring soup kitchens and needle exchange programs, job training and small opera companies to America's communities in the faces of those who champion tax breaks for the wealthy. Do we really think the new technology, or lack thereof, is going to stop THEM?"

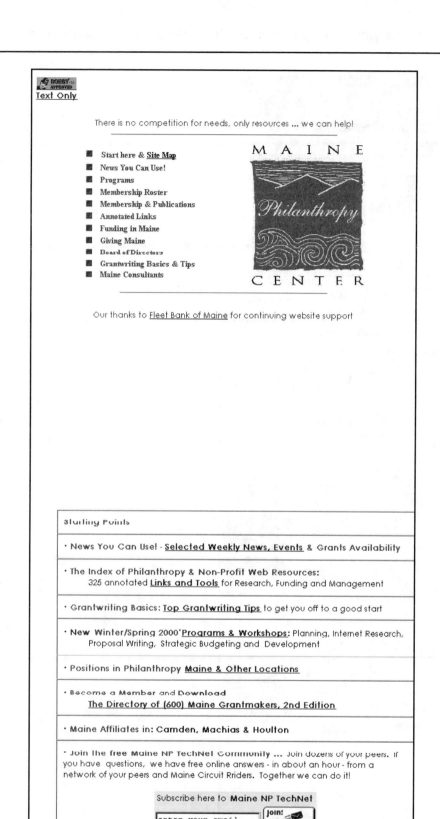

The Maine Center for Philanthropy home page at http://www.megrants.org. Reprinted with permission.

The CNET home page at http://www.cnet.com. Reprinted with permission from CNET, Inc. © copyright 1995-1999.

Chapter 9

Publicizing Your Site

Introduction

You can have the most professionally designed, comprehensive site in the world, but if no one knows about it, it will have no value to either your organization or its intended audience. Just as in sales of products, publicity and marketing are more than half of the battle.

Push vs. Pull

Push refers to strategies that enable content providers to automatically "push" information to users of their service. Examples include electronic mailing lists and e-zines that people have signed up for. Note that "push technology" has come to refer to broadcasts of custom-designed information that subscribers pay for, such as a summary of their favorite team's last game or the price of their favorite stocks.

Pull requires a user to take the initiative to acquire the information. Examples might be putting content on your Web site, such as a chat room, online courses, downloadable software or graphics, viewer surveys, or contests. Sending e-mail (or snail mail) to entice potential viewers to visit, having a banner ad on a related Web site heralding your own Web site, or linking your site to other sites are examples.

In marketing your Web site, it is often productive to think in terms of these two forms, one principally active and one principally passive from the perspective of the targeted audience, and use both forms to market your site.

Advertising

There are two reasons nonprofit organizations with e-commerce sites need to have a basic understanding of how advertising on the World Wide Web is different from conventional advertising.

First, Web advertising is a potential source of significant revenue for nonprofit organizations. This revenue may come from direct advertising by businesses, with charities posting banner advertisements of commercial products and services, just as many nonprofits accept commercial advertisements in their printed newsletters and magazines. Or it may come in the form of indirect advertising, as commercial companies recognize the value of being associated with a charity, and agree to sponsor the organization's Web site. This entails placing the company's logo on the site, with perhaps a subtle link to its home page near the bottom of the organization's page, in exchange for a hefty donation. Thousands of companies are comfortable with sponsoring charitable fundraisers, and many see Web site sponsorship as simply an extension of what they are already doing to participate in philanthropy. Others are motivated by the exposure their company gets from viewers who will click on the link to their site. As mentioned on page 53, the IRS is raising its eyebrows in response to this form of corporate sponsorship.

Second, the Web is becoming an advertising medium of choice for nonprofit organizations who want to reach a particular target market. Rather than (or in addition to) being a seller of Web-based advertising and sponsorships, nonprofit organizations are themselves advertising on the Web. Sometimes nonprofits are paying for this service. To an increasing degree, commercial Web sites are accepting the banner ads of charities for free placement on their pages, the Web equivalent of a "public service announcement."

Both phenomena are likely to grow, and Web advertising is likely to consume an increasing share of marketing budgets. The reason is becoming obvious when one looks at the trends.

Trend one: More and more people are becoming connected to the Internet. The gender gap has disappeared. While there continues to be an income disparity between those who are connected and those who are not (the so-called "Digital Divide"), this means that those who are on the Web are more likely to be young, highly educated, have a large amount of disposable income, and be comfortable with impulse buying and making purchases on the Web.

Trend two: The amount of time people are spending on the World Wide Web is increasing, and they are using the Internet as their primary source of information.

Trend three: Study after study (see reports put out by Neilson/Commerce Net, Forrester Research and the Graphic, Visualization and Usability Center of Georgia Tech) is documenting that the time people are devoting to surfing the Internet was formerly spent watching television—the traditional source of most advertising revenue in marketing budgets.

Research is also demonstrating that Web advertising is effective. A 1996 study by Millward Brown International found that a single exposure of a banner ad was more effective in increasing brand awareness than a single exposure to a print or television ad.

Some of the issues nonprofits need to be aware of with respect to selling or buying Web site advertising are the following:

1. *Pricing.* The money spent for Internet advertising is still doubling every year (increasing from about $267 million in 1996 to perhaps two billion dollars in 1999). There is no reason not to see some of these revenues being used to fund nonprofit organizations. But what should you charge for a commercial Web advertisement? A general rule of thumb is to charge $30-$40 for every thousand viewers who will see a banner ad. Commercial advertising has not yet become an accepted practice by many nonprofit organizations, many of whom prefer to accept sponsors for a Web site in which the sponsor makes a "donation" to the charity in exchange for putting the company logo on the pages with an acknowledgment of sponsorship—with perhaps a link to the home pages of the sponsors (see http://www.redcross.org).

2. *Size and structure of advertisements/banners.* The advertising industry is attempting to standardize the size of banner Web advertisements. One such system can be found at the Internet Advertising Bureau's Web site (http://www.iab.net). A full banner is 468 x 60 pixels. A half banner is 234 x 60 pixels, a button is 120 x 90 or 120 x 60 pixels, and a micro button is 88 x 31 pixels. There are some intermediate sizes included. To create a banner, you can use a standard graphics program (such as Adobe Photoshop) and create a sized graphic based on this standard. You save the file in JPEG or GIF format, which can be placed into HTML files. Web page development software can be used to turn the banner or button into a link that will transport the person who clicks on it to the advertiser's Web site.

3. *How the audience of an ad is measured.* As previously mentioned, hit counters do not tell the whole story. For advertisers, knowing how many people saw the advertisement is critical. The advertising industry is also attempting to standardize ways to measure Web site audiences. The Internet Advertising Bureau's Media Measurement Task Force proposed voluntary guidelines on standard page view, page visit, and page request metrics. The Web page for more information about this issue can be found at: http://www.iab.net).

Starting Your Own Mailing List

Starting an electronic mailing list is an example of using push strategies to promote pull strategies. One method professionals use to drive traffic to their Web site is to put information and advertising about new features on their sites, in addition to the general information provided on the mailing list. Some nonprofits also generate revenue by selling commercial advertisements on their mailing lists (see pages 51-53 on UBIT considerations).

Among the decisions you need to make when starting a list are:

1. What is the general topic?

2. Who is your audience? Professionals? Volunteers? The general public? The quality of your list is often dependent on how differenti-

ated the audience is from competing lists, but you need a critical mass of participants, not simply lurkers, to make the list lively and provocative.

3. Will it be a two-way (interactive discussion) list in which subscribers can post their content to the list, or a one-way electronic newsletter format?

4. What software will you use to generate the list? You have a choice of using software that lets you administer the list yourself (e.g., Majordomo, Listserv), or using commercial services that do almost all of the work (see http://www.egroups.com and http://www.listbot.com) but which may add advertising to the messages.

5. Will the list be moderated? On a moderated list, messages that are off topic, off color, or simply "off" can be deleted before being sent to the list. The list moderator can unilaterally decide that a discussion is getting out of hand, and can simply announce that no more messages about the topic will be permitted. The disadvantage is that some may feel there is inappropriate censorship. Also, moderating a list can be hard work, and painful if you decide you want to go on an African safari for six weeks.

6. What will be included in the Code of Conduct and netiquette? See the Code of Conduct for online communities in Appendix G for ideas to consider in your code of conduct. For example, what level of commercialization, if any, is acceptable?

7. How will you publicize the list?

8. What will be in the FAQ?

For general information about how to participate in an electronic mailing list, see Appendix F.

Other Strategies to Promote More Site Visits

1. Offer something free on your site, such as a newsletter, report on an issue, or a custom-designed screen saver that promotes your organization's niche.

2. Provide a weekly e-mail survey and post the results.

3. Have contests, with prizes being products sold on your site, such as organizational T-shirts, mugs, magazines, or tickets to events.

4. Have online events, such as having a local celebrity or your board chair participate in an online chat.

Selection and Registration of Domain Names

Every computer connected to the Internet has a unique Internet Protocol (IP) address. These addresses look like four numbers, separated by a period (207.44.25.233, for example). When you connect to another computer over the Internet, your computer needs to know the IP. However, IPs are too difficult to remember, for the most part. A system has been developed to provide more memorable addresses, called domain names. Once you get used to this system, domain names become easy to remember. In addition, you can tell a lot from the domain name—the type of organization, the geographical location, and often the name of the user. A domain name is the part of the Internet address after the "@" sign. For example, my personal e-mail address is:

gary.grobman@paonline.com.

Paonline is my Internet Service Provider (ISP), and ".com" indicates that it is a commercial provider. However, I could, for a fee, have this changed to:

gary.grobman@nonprofitecommerce.com, assuming no one else has taken the domain name "nonprofitecommerce.com" already.

Most domain name suffixes tell you something about the type of organization, and the last extension often indicates the country code for addresses outside of the United States.

Domain names make Web site addresses easy to read and remember. Let's say you are setting up a Web site, and your Web space is being provided by a company called "Yourweb." Yourweb is a reseller for space on a server at "Myweb." Your site's URL may look like this:

http://www.myweb.com/~yourweb/yourorganization/home.html

If Yourweb allows its customers to have "virtual domain" space, your site's URL could be shortened to the easier-to-remember and more distinctive:

http://www.yourorganization.org

There are fees for registering a virtual domain. Many organizations find the cost well worth it. Domain names are registered through Network Solutions (*http://www.networksolutions.com*) and other companies that have been approved as registrars, such as register.com (*http://www.register.com*) and TuCows (http://www.tucows.com).

Fees are typically $35 annually, although some sites may offer promotional discounts. These fees are in addition to the fees charged by your provider(s) for hosting your site.

Applications must be submitted electronically, by filling out a template on the Web site of the registrar you are using. You will need your name and address, the domain name you want to use (e.g., yourname.org) and the primary and secondary server Internet protocol number, which you can obtain from your ISP or Web space provider. Names are assigned on a first-come, first-served basis and are checked for prior use and for whether they are in some way objectionable. If this sounds too complicated, check with your server or your Web host. Many will do this work for an additional fee, and some include it when you sign up.

In choosing a domain name, you want something that is easy to remember, easy to identify with your organization, and easy to guess if your domain name is unknown (e.g. www.yourorg.org).

Search Engines and Directories

A search engine is a computer program that searches the Internet, or a large database of material from the Internet, and finds matches for keywords. A directory is analogous to a library card catalog, which organizes information you can find on the Internet by pre-selected categories With practice, you will develop a sense for when to use each.

Understanding how search engines work is critical to your marketing success. According to a Web page published by IMT Strategies (*http://www.imtstrategies.com/trendroom11.htm)*, most people will find your Web site through the use of a search engine. The research showed that people find Web sites in the following *ways:*

Search Engines: 46%
Word-of-mouth: 20%
Random Surfing: 20%
Magazine ads: 4.4%
"By accident":2.1%
TV spots: 1.4%
Targeted e-mail: 1.2%
Banner ads: 1%

Among the more popular search engines are:

Yahoo! (http://www.Yahoo.com)
Lycos (http://www.lycos.com)
Infoseek (http://www.infoseek.com)
Alta Vista (http://altavista.com)
Google (http://www.google.com)
Ask Jeeves (http://www.Askjeeves.com), which is a search engine of search engines
Northern Light (http://www.northernlight.com)
Dogpile (http://www.dogpile.com)

PhilanthropySearch, a search engine specifically targeted to serving nonprofit organizations, located at: http://www.philanthropysearch.com, is operational. It hasn't shown itself to be better than any of the general commercial search engines and directories, although its banner advertising is geared more to a nonprofit sector audience.

Users access a search engine by connecting to its Web address and then filling out an online form with the term or terms to search for.

What are some of the differences in search engines? In part, this is a hard question to answer, since they are always under development, changing, and improving. One major difference among the search engines is in what is being searched—Web page headers, all Web page text, newsgroups, or gopher, to give some examples.

One of the newer and more useful search engines, Google.com, provides some information on its site about how it works. For an inside peek, surf to:

http://www.google.com/why_use.html

Search engines usually provide a procedure for registering a new Web page with them so it will appear in searches. Nonprofits that develop their own Web pages should register their pages with as many search engines as they identify. There are one-stop service agencies which, for a fee, will register your site with scores of search engines.

Metatags

Metatags are keywords inserted into your HTML file that don't appear to the viewer of the page, but are found by search engines. Having appropriate metatags in your files makes it more likely that your page will be found by those who use the search engine to search on a particular key word.

Web Rings

If you are hoping to find a number of related sites on a particular topic, you might try searching the *Web Ring* site *(http://www.webring.org)*, which has a searchable database of more than 80,000 rings. Web Rings are linked groups of sites on a related topic. When you go to a site that is associated with a Web Ring, you will find an area, usually at the bottom of the site's home page, where you can click to go to the next site in the ring, the previous site, a random site in the ring, or a list of all sites in the ring. Web Rings have been developed on mental health, domestic violence, AIDS, homelessness, disabilities, premature babies, cancer, and numerous other topics. In late 1997, Thomas Cleereman started the *Social Work Web Ring (http://www.webring.org/cgi-bin/webring?ring=800290;list)*, which by May 2000 included 79 sites. The Web Ring site itself also provides information on starting a Web Ring.

Measuring Your "Hits"

Pete Rose retired in 1986 as the major league's all-time leader in hits with 4,256. There is no dispute about the number of hits he had, although the convention is that the hundreds of hits he had in exhibition games, All-Star games, League Championship series, and the World Series, are not counted in this total. Measuring the number of hits on your Web site is not as scientific. When someone tells you that their Web site registered 1,000 hits today, it could mean:

1. The number whose computers requested a file transfer (so that one person accessing your home page may be registering 20 hits because each of the 19 image files on your home page generated a separate file transfer).

2. That same person visited eight different pages on your site, but scrolled back and forth between two in order to keep from having his or her server time out.

Both of the above scenarios cause your hits to be increased. Other factors distort your hits in the other direction. Readers visit your site, and the HTML file is stored in the cache file of the browser. When the visitor revisits and doesn't "refresh," the file is retrieved from the browser and not over the Internet. Your hit counter doesn't record the hit. Or if you are counting unique visitors using sophisticated market analysis software, two users from the same network will show up as having the same computer.

Using cookies or having passwords eliminates some of this confusion, but most nonprofit organizations are not going to be concerned about these.

The point of this is that you need to take information about page hits with a grain of salt. Obviously, having more hits is better than less hits. Having a hit counter for each page does provide information that is definitely better than having no information.

That being said, you can find free hit counters at:

BeSeen (http://www.beseen.com/hitcounter/index.html)
BraveNet Web Services (http://www.bravenet.com/samples/counter.php)

For an online listing and review of free and other online hit counters, visit: Brian's Guide To Web Page Hit Counters (http://www.zoomnet.net/~skeppler/).

Up Close:

Rob Vandenberg, Founder, CEO and President LocalVoice

Rob Vandenberg founded LocalVoice with Suzanne Roberts in November 1998. The San Francisco-based company has become one of the best-known Application Service Providers (ASPs) targeting its services to charities. These companies provide software applications that offer online services such as fundraising, ticketing, membership-renewal, e-mail marketing, e-surveys, donor management applications, auctions, and Web site building.

LocalVoice provides a full range of easy-to-use, Web-based services to its clients that enable online relationship-building. The company's Web-based applications empower member-supported organizations to "push" customized, personalized content to their members, drive member traffic to the organization's Web site, build unique profiles of individual members and member populations as a whole, and activate secure online transaction processing.

Rob's interest in charitable fundraising was sparked by his experiences on the Board of Directors of the San Francisco YMCA.

"I was placed in charge of the organization's fundraising, giving me front-line exposure to some of the challenges and inefficiencies in attempting to raise money," he says. "It was this experience, coupled with my knowledge of e-commerce and the Internet, which led me to be a co-founder of LocalVoice. While full of potential and value for nonprofit organizations, e-commerce alone is an empty promise without the right tools and expertise."

Rob recognized early in his nonprofit board career that most charities were not equipped to take full advantage of using the Internet to perform their missions and raise money.

"Current technology advancements offer a wide variety of potential uses to charitable organizations," he points out. "However, these organizations have a history of lacking the financial and staffing resources to take advantage of cutting-edge technology." He asserts that ASPs focus on these technologies and create application packages that are specifically useful for this market, and offer their powerful solutions at affordable prices with security that is often superior to that otherwise accessible to the charity. "Just because a 'Donate Now' button resides in cyberspace does not make people any more compelled to contribute to an organization," he contends.

As examples, he points to some of his firm's clients who have successfully harnessed the Web for fundraising. Ohio Wesleyan University (http://www.owu.edu) is now driving all its alumni to give to their annual fund online. "OWU tells its alums that, through LocalVoice, they save a considerable amount of overhead on gift processing and administrative costs," he reports. In addition, this allows OWU Alumni to give on their own time, on their own terms, using their credit cards. Another client, Contra Costa Humane Society, broke its record for donations received during the 1999 holiday season. On a television spot at the end of a local broadcast, representatives told viewers to go to the CC Humane Web site and give—and viewers responded.

Unlike some of its competitors, LocalVoice charges a flat fee rather than collect a percentage of the donations it receives. "Thus, our clients pay us for the services we provide them and reap the entire reward of the success they achieve through the use of our applications," he acknowledges.

Rob is a fervent advocate for Web-based fundraising, and he points out five distinct advantages with this medium.

"The first advantage that makes the Internet attractive for fundraising is its broad reach, providing a cost-effective way to reach a large audience," he begins. "Other outreach methods, such as direct mail and telemarketing, are quite costly and difficult to measure. Using the power of the Internet, organizations can intelligently allocate their resources, deliver content that is pertinent to different segments of their constituency, and quantify the results of their work using specialized measurement software.

"Second, the Web enables efficient data management. Utilizing online data management tools allow directors of development, CEOs, alumni directors, and others involved in constituency relations the ability to access securely mission-critical data from any Internet connection. Using the package we provide, a director of development could monitor securely the progress of an ongoing fundraising campaign from the Internet connection at his or her office desk, at a hotel conference room, or even from the beach," he marvels.

"Third, the Internet is more convenient to members and donors than conventional communication. Rather than sending members a direct mailer that is the equivalent of a bill, or bothering them during dinnertime with a telephone call, the Internet empowers members to give on their own time and on their own terms. The data show that the results of this style of communication are positive—average online donations are roughly $130, whereas average direct mail donations are roughly $30.

"Fourth, the Internet provides the ability to develop one-on-one relationships. Just because a 'donate now' button resides in cyberspace does not make people any more compelled to contribute to an organization. Using powerful applications such as our firm's e-mail marketing engine, organizations can target specific members and serve these individuals customized e-mail messages. As the Internet matures, users expect to get useful information in an expedient fashion. The ability to serve up fresh content through e-mail and updated Web materials allows organizations the ability to engage their members on a personal level.

"And, fifth, the Internet provides a way to reach the younger generation. The average age of an online donor is 35 years old—decades younger than the average respondent to a direct mail appeal. The Internet allows charitable organizations the opportunity to engage younger individuals and to engender a sense of philanthropic spirit. Communication with this generation is increasingly important because many treat their donations as investments."

What advice does he give to the nonprofit executive who is ready to roll up her sleeves and get in on the e-commerce action?

"Start now," he says bluntly. "Outsource Internet services to companies that are designed to serve their market and to integrate the Internet into their organization's overall mission. Working with a company that understands both the Internet and your market space will allow you to save money and acquire a complete solution that integrates with your existing fundraising, contact management, and marketing, systems.

What is the future of Internet fundraising? Rob sees a rosy future ahead.

"The Chronicle of Philanthropy estimates that 25% of charitable donations will be raised online by 2008. That equals $100 billion dollars! The Internet will not take the place of 'conventional' fundraising methods; rather, it will work in conjunction with these methods and have a major impact on charitable organizations as a whole."

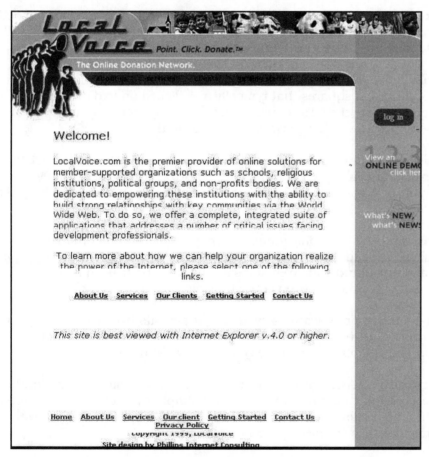

The LocalVoice home page at http://www.localvoice.com.
Reprinted with permission.

Appendix A: Glossary of E-Commerce and Internet Terms

404—The error message that appears when you click on a hypertext link and the URL referenced by the link does not exist.

Affiliate Program—an arrangement by which a person or organization receives a commission on sales generated by links from a Web site to the Web site of a vendor.

AltaVista—A popular and free search engine on the World Wide Web.

ASCII file—A file that contains only letters, numbers, and standard punctuation symbols from the American Standard Code for Information Exchange character set, and is the standard for the exchange of information between computer programs that may otherwise be incompatible. ASCII files do not contain formatting codes (such as those indicating that text is bold or italicized).

Backoffice—refers to the administrative and logistical functions carried out transparently by a third party, such as data collection, order fulfillment, customer service, inventory, and payment processing.

Banner Ad—Advertisements on a Web site that generally consist of colorful rectangles or squares that typically are clicked on to direct the viewer to the Web site of the ad's sponsor. These ads may include animations and "teaser" copy to encourage viewers to click on them.

Browser—A computer program that permits access to the World Wide Web by reading and interpreting HTML files. A browser may be text-only (such as Lynx), or graphical (such as Netscape Navigator or Microsoft® Internet Explorer).

Certificate—An electronic security form provided by an authorized security software vendor that serves as a digital "passport,"certifying information about you and your Web site so that it can be trusted by those who send encrypted data to you via the Internet.

Chat—A telecommunications system that permits two or more people to use their keyboards to communicate in real time and engage in "conversations." The chatters view on their monitors what each types in.

Click-to-Give—A business model that enables a Web site viewer to authorize a charitable donation by a sponsor simply by clicking on a banner within a Web site. The clicker often receives a "thank you" along with a commercial advertisement or commercial banner.

Commercial Service Provider—A commercial company (such as AOL, CompuServe, or Microsoft® Network) that provides an Internet connection as well as online content (such as forums, chat, news, and other information and files) that is accessible only to its subscribers.

Content—Refers to the information (in the form of text, graphics, music, video, or other media) that is available at a Web site.

Cookie—A text file sent to your browser directory by some Web sites that contains information useful to such sites, and which can be accessed each time you revisit the site. Most cookies are of some benefit to both the Web site and the visitor.

Counter—A software program that tracks the number of accesses or hits to a Web page.

Cyberspace—The virtual space in which electronic communication by computers takes place, including the physical and metaphysical residence of e-mail, Web sites, and other Internet communication modalities.

Digital Divide—The term recognizing that there are differences in the access to the Internet based on gender, ethnicity, and income level. The gender gap has disappeared since 2000, but the other gaps have remained.

Domain name—The part of the Internet address that identifies the specific organization being communicated with and converts the numerical Internet Protocol addresses into names with letters, which can be more easily remembered.

E-Commerce—As used in this book, business transactions conducted over the Internet.

E-mail (electronic mail)—Messages that arrive on your computer from other computers through the telephone lines via a data connection from the Internet or an Intranet or other network.

E-Philanthropy—Fundraising utilizing the Internet.

E-Zine—A magazine or newsletter that is published using the Internet rather than in print.

Encryption—Disguising messages for security purposes by using cryptography "keys" that permit only the sender and receiver to decode them. Those without the correct keys see only gobbledygook.

FAQ (Frequently Asked Questions)—A file of questions and answers found in Usenet Newsgroups, Web pages, and other Internet-related documents that is prepared to assist new participants. May be pronounced "fack" or "F-A-Q."

File—A set of computer-generated information, such as a document, database, or Web page, that is identified by a unique name and is created, transferred, copied, or downloaded/uploaded as a distinct unit. Files are stored on hard disks or other storage media, and are organized by using directories and subdirectories.

Firewall—protective software installed on a computer network for the purpose of preventing unauthorized access to certain files inside the network.

Flame—An electronic message that contains abusive, denigrating, threatening, or inciting language, and is often directed to those deemed by the sender(s) to have violated the informal rules of Internet conduct.

Freenet—A type of Bulletin Board Service (BBS) that provides free (usually), community-based information and downloadable files, and inexpensive or free access to the Internet and e-mail.

Freeware—Software programs that are available free for public use.

GIF (Graphic Image File)—The most popular format for graphics files on the World Wide Web. The file extension *.gif* is used for these files.

Hit—A count each time someone accesses a file on the Web. The term also refers to the number of matches a search engine accesses in response to a search term.

Home page—The World Wide Web page that is intended as the entry point to an entire Web site of an identifiable person or group (it may also be the *only* page on a one-page site). It usually includes introductory and identifying information, as well as links to the rest of the site's pages. It also refers to the page that appears on your browser when you first open the browser.

Host—The computer that makes its files and data available to other computers and is directly connected to the Internet. An Internet host is the computer that serves as the intermediary from the Internet to the consumer end-user.

HTML (Hyper Text Markup Language)—The programming language for World Wide Web pages, which consists of coded tag pairs using symbols from the ASCII character set, formatting documents for the World Wide Web.

Hyperlink—A part of a Web page that is coded so that when a viewer clicks on it, he/she is taken to another Web page, and can navigate back and forth between these pages. Viewers see the hyperlink as text or a graphic that is bold, underlined, or a different color, and that, depending on the browser, indicates it is a link by a change in the icon that appears when the pointing device's cursor is on it.

Internet—The system in which millions of computers worldwide are linked for the purpose of electronic mail, mailing lists, newsgroups, and the World Wide Web.

Internet Service Provider (ISP)—A business that makes the Internet accessible to consumers via a dial-up service to a local number.

JAVA—A programming language that supports animations and other sophisticated special effects on World Wide Web pages.

JPEG—A format for World Wide Web page graphics. The file extension *.jpg* is used for these files.

Keys—Encryption files that must be in the correct format in order for an encrypted file to be viewed.

Keyword—A word used by an online service that serves as a gateway to files, chat, newsgroups, news, and other Internet content related to that word. It also refers to a word searched by search engines to find Internet files and pages.

Link—A reference to a file or Web page placed in an HTML file that, when clicked on using an Internet browser, takes the viewer directly to that Web page or file. (See also *hyperlink*.)

Listserv®—Commercially developed mailing list software that permits the management of e-mail mailing lists.

Lurk—To observe postings in mailing lists, newsgroups, or chat discussions without actively participating. Lurking is recommended before active participation.

Lycos—A popular, free search engine on the Internet.

Mailing lists—A system that permits Internet users to subscribe to an e-mail discussion group that is topical, and to post a message that will be automatically sent to all other subscribers of that list. The software that manages these lists is usually either Listserv® or MajorDomo.

MajorDomo—A freeware mailing list management program manager that uses the UNIX operating system.

Netiquette—Internet etiquette, a set of unwritten (for the most part) rules that have developed in the Internet culture and serve as rules of conduct.

Newbie—An inexperienced Internet user who is not familiar with netiquette or FAQ files, and who often annoys experienced users, all of whom were once newbies.

Online—Being connected through the telephone lines to another computer.

Online Charity Auction—An auction that is conducted over the Internet, and that may include items donated by celebrities that are considered valuable even to people who have little interest in the mission of the sponsoring charity.

Online Community—A group of people who interact online, such as by joining a newsgroup, mailing list, chat room, or a Web site that integrates all of these services.

Online Shopping Mall—Software that creates a virtual store consisting of two or more retailers that pay commissions to the manager of the mall and often provide charitable donations based on the amount of purchases from consumers.

Pixel—the basic unit of programmable color on a computer screen. Its physical size depends on the resolution of the screen.

Public domain—Intellectual property (such as software, books, clip art) that is not copyrighted, and can be freely copied and distributed without paying royalties to the creator.

Pull—A marketing technique that requires a user to take some action in order to access Internet content, such as by visiting a World Wide Web site and clicking on a specific link.

Push—A marketing technique that delivers content over the Internet that doesn't require a user to actively request it each time, such as a mailing list.

Push Technology—Webcasting technology, such as Pointcast, Bongo, and Netscape's Inbox direct service, that provides customized information to subscribers based on their profiles and interests.

Real Time—Communication between or among Internet users that occurs simultaneously, such as through chat, as contrasted to the exchange of e-mail.

Search engine—A computer program that searches a database (which may contain millions of World Wide Web pages) or the World Wide Web itself and that is accessed by filling out an online form with a word or phrase to be searched, and parameters relating to the format of the answer the user desires.

Server—A computer that makes services available on a network.

Shareware—Computer programs that are made available free-of-charge on a trial basis, with an address to send a fee if the user likes it or wishes to purchase upgrades or additional software.

Snail mail—Communications sent via the U.S. Postal Service.

Spam—Large numbers of inappropriate or otherwise undesirable e-mail messages, including bulk commercial messages (also called "junk e-mail"). When used as a verb, refers to the process of generating hundreds or thousands of such messages to a violator of netiquette as a form of punishment, or to sending bulk junk e-mail.

SSL (Secure Socket Layer)—The dominant method of encryption used to send secure files over the World Wide Web.

Surf—To navigate through the World Wide Web by following interesting links.

URL (uniform resource locator)—A unique address on the Internet.

Virus—A computer program, designed as a prank or sabotage, that modifies or destroys the victim's computer capabilities. A virus is uploaded to the victim's computer by deception.

Webmaster—The individual who designs or administers a Web site.

Web page—An individual file/document at a Web site, which has a unique address and appears when you click on the hypertext link coded with that address or when you type the address into your browser.

Web site—A collection of related and linked Web pages that is developed by one entity. Typically, a Web site has a home page that directs readers to other pages within the site using hyperlinks.

World Wide Web—A feature of the Internet that uses files containing hypertext links, which permit the viewer to navigate among potentially millions of computer hosts by clicking on the part of the computer screen that shows those links.

Yahoo!—A popular Internet search engine and directory (stands for "You Always Have Other Options").

Appendix B: A Short Course on Copyright Issues

Copyright owners are granted the exclusive rights to reproduce a work, to modify it (such as by creating what is termed a "derivative" work), to distribute it, and to perform or otherwise show it to the public. A copyright is a government-sanctioned legal right (referenced in the U.S. Constitution in Article I, Section 8) for the creator of a work to maintain the exclusive right to copies and/or publication of that work. It is federal law, and thus the rights associated with copyrights do not vary among the states. The work must be something tangible and creative. Thus, it can't be an idea, nor can it be a collection of facts (although if the way a collection of facts is put together is itself creative, then this compilation can be eligible for copyright protection). But it can be a photograph, a Usenet posting, a piece of art, or this book. No special registration is required for a work to be copyrighted.

This legal protection is bestowed automatically on every work created in the United States after April 1, 1989. This means that even if you see a document on a Web site (or anywhere else) that lacks the copyright symbol, it is still copyright-protected, unless the creator explicitly states that the work is intended to be in the public domain.

There are, are course, legal advantages to formally registering a work with the Copyright Office (with a $30 fee), and registration is necessary in the event that you want to recover economic damages from copyright infringement.

A copyright lasts until 50 years after the work's creator dies. This means that you could post the entire set of Shakespeare's plays on a Web page (as has been done) and not have to worry about copyright infringement.

Prior to the ratification of the North American Free Trade Agreement and the Uruguay Round Agreements Act (P.L. 103-465), once a work was in the public domain, the creator could never regain the copyright rights. These two documents provided some exceptions.

It makes sense to use a copyright symbol on works you want protected, although in theory, this is not really necessary. This is done by putting on the work a © (insert year of copyright) by (insert name of creator). If you are truly risk-averse concerning the work, you should register it with the Copyright Office.

You can't legally take photographs or cartoons from magazines without prior permission and scan them for use in your organization's Web page.You can be charged with infringement whether you use a work for commercial or non-commercial purposes, although the purpose could affect the damages that could be recovered from you by the creator of the work.

Copyright protection is not absolute. For example, under the "fair use" doctrine, a person may, without permission, make limited use of portions of a work. This often occurs in quoting one book for use in another, or making copies of part of a work to distribute in schools, for example. This doctrine, as interpreted by the Register of Copyrights in a 1961 report, permits limited use of copyrighted material used in the "quotation of excerpts in a review or criticism for purposes of illustration or comment; quotation of short passages in a scholarly or technical work, for illustration or clarification of the author's observations; use in a parody of some of the content of the work parodied; summary of an address or article, with brief quotations, in a news report; reproduction by a library of a portion of a work to replace part of a damaged copy; reproduction by a teacher or student of a small part of a work to illustrate a lesson; reproduction of a work in legislative or judicial proceedings or reports; incidental and fortuitous reproduction, in a newsreel or broadcast, of a work located in the scene of an event being reported."

In most cases, the quote or excerpt must be attributed to the creator, and must be such that the commercial value of the work is not harmed.

Public domain

This term refers to works that are not protected by copyright. It includes works created before copyright protection existed, works created by government employees in the scope of their employment, works once protected by copyright that has since expired, simple facts and figures, and works that the creator permits to be in the public domain.

For the most part, creators of works desire to have their works seen by as many people as possible. If you want to put something on your Web site that is the work of another person, it makes sense to simply ask him or her for permission (but get this in writing, even if it is an e-mail message response). If the creator is not willing to grant permission for free, the offer of a few dollars may make the difference. If it is an article written by a college professor, it certainly has a better chance of getting free permission than if the work was written by a free-lance writer who makes a living from, in part, electronic distribution of his or her work.

When in doubt, ask. Copyright infringement law is changing; what once was restricted to the civil damages arena is slowly evolving to the criminal arena, and some violations are likely to be felonies by the time you read this. Even if you win a case, the risk is time, legal resources, and a lot of sleepless nights.

Appendix C: Web Site Hosting

In our 1998 book, *The Nonprofit Internet Handbook*, Gary Grant and I provide in some detail a listing of what one needs to connect to the Internet. The typical requirements are a computer and monitor, a modem, or other technology to transport data from the Internet to your computer, a telephone line, an Internet Service Provider (ISP), and communications and other software. I will assume that you are this far along technologically, but that you may still have some questions about how to establish your own Web site capable of serving as your organization's virtual store.

Before setting up a new Web site, it is critical to decide which server to use. The server is the computer where your Web site files physically reside. It should be accessible 24 hours a day, and some of the decisions you make about your site will be based on the technical specifications relating to the host server. You have several choices with respect to choosing a server:

1. *In-house server.* If you work at a university, there will likely be a server available for you to use through the campus computing center. Likewise, if you work for a large nonprofit organization, there may be resources to set up an in-house computer as a Web server.

2. *An online service.* Many commercial Internet service providers, such as America Online (AOL), offer their subscribers space for a small Web site, included in the subscription price. (Check to see whether you are permitted to use such a site for commercial purposes, and determine if you desire to do so if this use is permitted.)

3. *Internet Service Provider.* Many local and national Internet service providers offer space for Web pages for their subscribers. There may be an additional fee, or the Web space may be included in the Internet access account fee. A growing trend is for these service providers to offer e-mail and World Wide Web access for free and finance their costs by selling advertising.

4. *Web-hosting services.* These are companies that specialize in making Web space available on their servers, often at reasonable prices or even for free. Many of these companies advertise in the back of computer magazines. Some commercial (and non-commercial) organizations offer nonprofit organizations free or reduced-fee space for home pages.

There are many organizations that provide free space for nonprofit organizations, or do so for a modest charge. There are directories available on the Internet that list hundreds of these.

I offer the following advice:

1. Look for a host in your local community. A searchable directory can be found at:

    http://www.lights.com/freenet compiled by Peter Scott (Northern Lights Internet Solutions).

2. Use a search engine or directory and search on the term "free Web pages" or "free Web-hosting" or "free Web space." When I did this in May 2000 using the Yahoo Directory, I was directed to scores of useful links, including a site that provides information about what the sponsors judge to be the top 100 free Web-hosting sites, along with capsule reviews (http://www.100best-free-web-space.com/index.htm).

   Also, consider checking out the following sites for information about free Web hosting:

   http://www.lights.com/freenet
   http://geocities.yahoo.com/home/
   http://xoom.com/home/

3. Contact your state association of nonprofit organizations. These associations are located in the state capitals of 35 states and the District of Columbia. If you need the e-mail address for the association in your state, e-mail me at: gary.grobman@paonoline.com or consult my book, *The Nonprofit Handbook* (Second Edition), which can be found in many public libraries.

4. Ask around. Find out what your colleagues have and what they think. You may want to pay a small monthly fee in order to have reliable and available technical support, a larger storage area for your files, easier access for updating, the availability of Web site construction tools, domain name services, and someone you can trust to be in business ten years from now. You may need to pay a fee in order to find a host capable of supporting encryption for your e-commerce transactions, or other specialized e-commerce software. By paying a fee, you are likely to be eligible for more services such as a bulletin board, guestbook, key word search engine, a links page, usage statistics, more disk space, and access to a secure server.

Some of the issues you need to resolve include the cost, limits on how many bytes are allowed for the Web site files, the process by which the files are updated (can you do this yourself from a remote computer, or do you upload the file to your ISP and the ISP puts it online when he or she gets around to it?), and whether the server provides you with a way to determine the number of "hits" and other statistics.

Some of the other issues you should consider when choosing a server include limits on commercial use, whether the server supports encryption software, whether access and availability is reasonable, extras offered, such as site counters and site search engines, and the availability of experienced technical support.

For the basics on designing a simple Web page, see Appendix D.

Appendix D: Basic Web Page Design

Step 1. Select your host server (see Appendix C).

Step 2. Determine the content and WWW Design.

What are you trying to communicate, and who is your audience? Are you willing to sacrifice the time required for users to access your page in exchange for lots of flashy graphics? Do you need to use animation, lots of color, and breathtaking graphics to attract visitors, or is plain vanilla information enough? What is the purpose of the site? To generate as much revenue as you can through donations and product sales? To attract clients or members? To identify new donors? To recruit volunteers? To provide a public service? All of the above?

If you create a site, consider whether others would want to visit it and why. Are you creating a site to ask for donations for your organization? If that is all, then do not be too surprised if you get few visitors. This is not to say that you cannot and should not seek donations on your Web site. You have to be a bit subtle about it. You perhaps need to include information resources that are beneficial to the visitor.

Typically, you will start with a home page that serves as a table of contents, with your logo, address, telephone number, e-mail address, and links to other Web pages—maybe one for each of the above purposes. To give you a head start on a constructive and efficient design, look at the pages of other organizations that you find attractive and effective. Then look at the source code, or HTML code, of those pages to see how they achieved the effect that you liked. Software, such as Web Fetch or Wing Flyer, is designed to capture all of the HTML source code that created a page (but beware, these files may be copyrighted). Even without this software, the HTML file of every page you view with your browser is captured byte for byte in a file in the cache, subdirectory of your communications program's directory. Since HTML is compatible with ASCII (which is the basis for text files), you can view these files in Windows Notepad or any word processing program. Simply open up the file in either of these programs.

Many Webmasters would be flattered if you compliment them on their site design and would not object if you request their permission to copy some of the design features of their site. Some might even offer to design your site for free, and others might provide their design for a token fee. If you are using Netscape Navigator as your browser, you can open the View menu and click on "Document Source" to see the coding for any page.

Step 3. Convert your files to HTML.

Inexpensive (or even free) software is available to convert conventional document files to HTML format. Two of the most popular Web page design programs are Adobe's PageMill (getting tougher to find these days) and Microsoft's Frontpage. Most modern word processing software (Microsoft's Word for Windows, any version higher than 7.0, for example) will let you save a word processed file in HTML format. You also can do it manually by placing HTML codes where they belong.

Each HTML file should include the following:

```
<HTML>
<HEAD><TITLE>Insert title here</TITLE></HEAD>
<BODY>insert rest of page here</BODY>
</HTML>
```

As you can see, HTML codes often are in pairs. There is a code at the beginning and a code at the end of words to which the code is applied. The beginning code is enclosed by an open caret and closed caret. The code at the end is enclosed by an open caret followed by a forward slash, and ends with a closed caret.

Background colors can be changed from the default white by placing codes within the <body> code. For example, using Body Bgcolor=A5 2A 2A will make the background brown.

Headings can be sized by adding the tag <hx>insert text here</hx>, where x is a positive whole number from 1 to 6 (small to large).

Paragraph/line breaks. A line break code (<br>) will start the text that follows on a new line without adding space above or below the line. A paragraph break code (<p>) will place the text that follows this code on a new line, with a space between the previous line and the new line, making a new paragraph. There is no need to put a line break at the end of each line within a paragraph—the lines will automatically wrap. The line break is used when you need a "hard return" after a partial line, such as in an address or a poem.

Other commonly used text codes include:

```
<center>insert text to be centered </center>
<b>insert text to be made bold</b>
<I>insert text to be italicized</I>
<font color="RGB" Size=n>insert text to have a font or color change
<Font> where RGB is the color code and n is a number between -7 and 7
which is greater or less than the baseline font size.
<blockquote>insert text here to be indented from both margins</blockquote>
<HR> creates a horizontal line
<HR WIDTH=X% Align=Y SIZE=Z> creates a line where x is the % proportion of page width, Y is the position (left, center or right), and Z is the thickness of the line.
```

Ordered lists are sequentially numbered items. The list is begun and ended by <OL>insert items to be listed</OL>. Each item that is part of the list is enclosed by the tag <LI>insert item</LI>. Using this tag places a number in front of each item.

Unnumbered lists are bulleted items. The list is begun and ended by <UL>insert items to be bulleted</UL>. Each item that is to be preceded by a bullet is tagged in the same way as an ordered list.

Step 4: Add Links

There are several basic kinds of links that appear on Web pages. Here is how some of these look in HTML code:

Links to a local file. This is a link to a file within the same directory (and within the same Web site) being linked from. It appears on the browser in a different color than other text. The tag for accomplishing this in the body of text is:

<A HREF="name of file.html">the text that you want to appear on the page</A>

Links to other HTML pages:
<A HREF="http://fullURL">name of page</A>
This type of link sends the viewer to another Web page, which can be within the same Web site or part of another site.

Links to e-mail:
<A HREF="MAILTO:gary.grobman@paonline.com">Send mail to Gary</A>
This type of link provides a form for the viewer to send e-mail to you or someone else in your organization.

Links to graphics files:
<IMG=SRC "nameofgraphicsfile.GIF" height=xxx width=yyy> where x and y are integers
This type of link puts a graphic on the Web page.

Step 5: Adds bells and whistles such as animations, forms, graphics, frames, search engines, links, and hit counters.

You can put together an attractive Web page without being any more sophisticated than using the above tags. For the more adventurous, there are languages other than HTML, such as JAVA, which are used to provide animations on your page.

There are plenty of reference books on how to design and construct a Web page (see For Further Reading section of this book).

There are also sites for World Wide Web clip art and CGI scripts (used as templates for guestbooks, counters, surveys, and other forms for your pages). Among them are:

Over the Rainbow (http://www.gininet.com)
Here, nonprofit organizations can download free icons, bullets, animations, clip art, backgrounds, and bars, "provided the organization encourages its members to visit my site."

Nuthin' But Links (http://www.nuthinbutlinks.com)
There are links to sites here where you can find HTML tutorials, Web page graphics, animated GIFs, tools for determining colors, JAVA resources, CGI scripts, counters, guestbooks, and almost anything else you may need to build and enhance the attractiveness of your Web site.

Barry's Clip Art Server (http://www.barrysclipart.com/)

This site has a searchable and indexed database of hundreds of downloadable, copyright-free images.

Web Site Design Tips

1. Frequently update the material on your site and make the content useful. Regardless of how "cool" your site looks, people won't return unless there is new information there on a regular basis.

2. Keep the design simple. People value their time. Graphics and special effects slow down browsers. Those who want to continually use your site don't want to have to search around each time because the design changes frequently. As a rule of thumb, design your pages such that they will load within 10 seconds.

3. Market what you are good at. If your organization's niche is in child advocacy, make your Web site the one-stop shopping place to find all of the information related to children, and don't stray too far from that.

4. If your organization depends on membership revenue, don't give out everything on your Web site. What is the incentive for individuals to become members if they receive the services for free just by logging into your site?

5. Don't put information on the Web that you would be embarrassed to find on the front page of your local newspaper. For example, if you are calling for advocacy on a certain bill, you may not want to disclose the strategy of the legislative coalition with which you are working.

6. Don't be shy about providing plenty of links to related sites, including your statewide and national affiliates, and government sources of information. Make sure links are clear and made in such a way as to not imply that the content at another site is your own. It is a good idea to let Webmasters know when you link to their sites. Most of them will be thrilled, and your notification will enable them to let you know if their sites move or if the URLs change. And don't give links such prominent placement on your page that you will lose your visitor immediately to the link.

7. Don't put everything on your home page. Use it as a Table of Contents and introduction rather than as the body of the Web site. Use links to take your site's visitors to internal files, such as your brochure, newsletter, message from the President, advocacy corner, board member list, and other files, and, of course, to your store.

8. Place a text line on the home page letting viewers know when the page was last updated.

9. Place links at the bottom of each Web page to return to the home page and to send e-mail to the Webmaster.

10. If possible, provide a place on the home page for a link to a text-only version of your pages. If you are using sophisticated animations or frames, the page may be inaccessible to those using older browsers.

11. Simplify your domain name as much as you can.

12. Publicize your site on all of the popular directories and search engines. Point your browser to these search engines for information on how to register your site.

13. Make sure that you do not post material that is copyrighted by others without obtaining written permission, and be sure to place a copyright notice on your own material on your Web site.

14. Consider placing a link on your site to free translation services, such as the one offered by AltaVista *(http://www.altavista.com)*. This service will translate your site (or a particular page of the visitor's choice) into several foreign languages, making it readable to a wider audience.

15. Make it as accessible as possible to as many people as possible. Visit the Center for Applied Special Technology (CAST) site (http://www.cast.org) for a free evaluation of the extent to which your site meets accessibility standards, or (http://www.w3.org/WAI/GL/) for the standards themselves.

16. Highlight important or new information on the home page.

17. Make the site professional, free of personal information.

18. Place detailed contact information prominently on the home page.

19. Don't overuse backgrounds and color; make sure content can be read from every popular browser. To test this, visit the Web Page Backward Compatibility Viewer, which can be found at: http://www.anybrowser.org/campaign.

20. Consider the links to be the same as adding content, assuring that each one adds to the site's value before including it.

Appendix E: Web Writing Issues

For nonprofit organizations, publishing documents on the Web is an effective strategy for reducing the costs of printing, postage, and processing requests for publications. But saving money is only one advantage. Publications can be updated easily and posted, which means that you no longer have to order, or throw out, so many brochures, reports, and other publications when they inevitably become out of date. When your publication is available in camera-ready format, you no longer have to wait days or weeks for it to be sent to a printer and come back printed and bound. It can appear on your Web site within minutes.

It is often a difficult decision to determine who should receive a conventionally printed report, and distribution is often limited because of cost considerations. Publishing the material on the Web permits everyone in the world with Web access (either from their own computer, their work computer, or institutions such as libraries and schools that provide Web access) to read your document. And even if you send me a copy of your organization's annual report in the mail, I may throw it out but then find that I need some information from it. Having it available on your Web site means I can access it immediately, even if I didn't throw out the report, but it is hidden in a stack of papers.

Many organizations have a "restricted access" feature for members, or their board, that denies access to the general public. Sensitive documents can be posted here for a pre-selected audience.

One additional, often overlooked, benefit of publishing material on a Web site is the feature of interactivity. Unlike conventional publishing, publishing on a Web site provides easy opportunities to obtain instant feedback from readers, either by clicking on a "mailto" link, or by filling out an electronic survey form.

To promote visits to your organization's Web site (which, if you want to promote e-commerce opportunities, you should be thinking about all of the time), you need to have content that is attractive to potential visitors. For most nonprofit organizations, that content is specific information that visitors will find useful and cannot obtain anywhere else.

But simply putting your newsletter word-for-word on your Web site, unedited for the Web, is a mistake.

Imagine how you might contrast two scenarios about someone reading your monthly newsletter. The first involves the person reading the version that you send in the mail, and the second is the version you post on your Web site. In the first scenario, the reader is likely to be holding the newsletter, sitting or reclining in a comfortable position in a well-lighted area, starting from the first word, and reading every word (or close to it). In the second scenario, the reader is sitting on a chair, poised in front of a flickering, low-resolution computer monitor, and skimming the content. How do we know the reader is skimming? Research by Jacob Nielsen and John Morkes (see http://www.useit.com/alertbox/9703b.html) demonstrates that reading on a computer screen is about 25% slower than reading conventionally, and as a result, only about 16% of Web page viewers read what is on the screen word-for-word.

This argues for a Web writing style that is different from that for "dead tree" publications. First, the articles need to be shorter, preferably in bite-sized morsels that can be seen in one screen. The text is written to facilitate scanning, such as having keywords in bold, and bulleted key points. Headings and subheadings are prominent; there is usually a single idea per paragraph, with space separating these ideas. Pull quotes (excerpts from the text which are important) may appear in sidebars with larger, more decorative fonts. Most important, ideas are expressed simply in short sentences, and article length overall is typically half of what would be appropriate for conventional publishing.

One convenient feature I have found on some Web pages with very short paragraphs of text and fancy graphics to illustrate them, linked in series, is the availability of a link to large articles unencumbered by graphics, labeled "printer-friendly version." The viewer reads from the series, but prints from the link without the graphics.

Here are ten writing tips for improving your Web pages:

1. Make all content compatible for scanning by the reader. Use bulleted lists and make key words bold.

2. Shorten content to 50% or less of what would appear in a printed publication.

3. Tailor content to needs of your Web audience. The language should be at the level of your audience. Technical requirements, such as using frames, search engines, and file format (e.g. HTML or PDF files) should be at the level of your audience

4. Take advantage of the Web's interactivity. Seek feedback from the audience by using surveys and "mailto" links to find out what features need to be improved, and what the audience particularly wants to see on your site.

5. Write in a conversational style. In contrast to traditional writing, sentence fragments are acceptable on Web pages. Colloquialisms are also considered acceptable, assuming the image you want to project is informal. Avoid the passive tense!

6. Limit paragraphs to a single idea/concept. Remember, most readers are skimming and looking for a key concept.

7. Keep sentences short. Any sentence over 20 words is likely to confuse.

8. Correct spelling is still important.

9. Make information your first priority, entertainment second. For almost all nonprofit Web sites, your organization is unlikely to be able to compete with commercial sites who draw their viewers with

entertainment. More likely, your viewers will visit your site because they want to know something about an issue on which your organization has expertise and credibility. Capitalize on this by giving the viewer what he/she wants. Flashy animations, jaw-dropping graphics, and slick cartoons are fine, but should be secondary on most nonprofit organizational sites.

10. Label buttons and links so your audience gets what it expects. Creating descriptions of labels, buttons, and links is a form of writing. Think of these as analogous to the newspaper headline—short and descriptive, and a clear, unambiguous summary of the content it seeks to describe.

Appendix F: Electronic Mailing Lists

So, you are clamoring for a quick, unbiased evaluation of fundraising software from those who have actually used it rather than those who developed it or market it. Or you need to find out what luck your colleagues around the world are having with direct solicitation of prospects by e-mail. Or perhaps you are seeking answers to, or opinions about, a myriad of other real-life dilemmas of a seasoned professional in the field.

You need practical advice, and you need it now, if not yesterday.

Increasingly, professionals in non-profit organizations are turning to the Internet for information, and Internet mailing list postings are becoming the tool of choice to connect those who have information and are willing to share it with those who need it. What makes these communication transactions even more attractive is that all of this is free, provided you have an e-mail account.

In our 1998 book *The Non-Profit Internet Handbook*, Gary Grant and I wrote that the Internet is "like having your own private library, entertainment center, news and clipping service, professional conference, private club, and nightly gala soirée." Internet mailing lists often achieve each of these objectives. Once you subscribe, usually by sending a simple e-mail with the word "subscribe," your e-mail address, and real name, you receive the "mail," a series of e-mail messages that subscribers to the list send that get broadcast to every subscriber on the list. These e-mails arrive in your Internet mail box either individually as each message is posted, or in a daily digest consisting of a single message that contains all of the posts for that day.

Some of these mailing lists are "moderated"; that is, each message is reviewed by a list supervisor for appropriateness before it is posted to all members of the list. Others are unmoderated, and members self-police the list by punishing those who transgress the list's netiquette by sending flame messages—personal e-mails disparaging the violators.

There has been a veritable explosion in the number and quality of these lists recently. Newly developed software, corporate sponsorship, and an explosion of Internet advertising have increased the ease by which anyone, regardless of technical expertise or money, can create a quality mailing list.

There are more than 90,000 Internet mailing lists in the Liszt database (http://www.liszt.com), perhaps a small fraction of those that are on the 'Net. More and more of these are devoted to nonprofit issues generally and charitable fundraising in particular.

You can find more than 40 mailing lists frequented by nonprofit board members and staff simply by pointing your Web browser to: *http://charitychannel.com/forums/*

Among the more popular lists for fundraisers are (in alphabetical order):

FundList (listproc@listproc.hcf.jhu.edu) subscribe FundList <firstname lastname>

Gift-Pl (listserv@indycms.iupui.edu) subscribe GIFT-PL, firstname lastname>

GiftManage (listserv@CharityChannel.com) subscribe GIFTMANAGE <firstname lastname>

PRSPCT-L (LISTSERV@Bucknell.EDU) subscribe PRSPCT-L <firstname lastname>

Online Fundraising (autoshare@gilbert.org) sub fundraising

Nonprofit Digest (nonprofit-request@rain.org) subscribe <firstname lastname>

To subscribe, send an e-mail to the Internet address in parentheses with a message in the body of the e-mail identical to what follows the parentheses, inserting your real first and last names for what is included between the caret symbols.

While most of these mailing lists are based in the United States, there are lists that specialize in discussions about fundraising in other countries. Among them are the United Kingdom-based *FundUK* (subscribe fundUK in the subject line, mail to: funduk-request@lists.dircon.co.uk); the German-based Spenden (subscribe spenden, firstname lastname, nameoforganization, mail to: majordomo@dsk.de), and the German-based International Philanthropy (International Philanthropy in the subject line, your e-mail address, first name, last name, title and organization in the message area; mail to: black@dsk.de).

I recommend several techniques to find sources of lists, new and established, that may interest you. First, information about many of the more popular mailing lists, including subscription information, can be found at Web sites such as Fundraising UK, Ltd (http://www.fundraising.co.uk/other_fr/lists.html) and The Management Center (http://www.tmcenter.org/library/npnewsgroups.html).

Second, you can search the Liszt Web site (http://www.liszt.com) by keyword. A recent search on the term "fundraising" resulted in eight matches, although some of these lists were no longer operational. Third, the popular newsletters (both print and online) and newspapers catering to professional nonprofit staff (such as *Contributions, Philanthropy Journal, Nonprofit Times,* and *Chronicle of Philanthropy*), also carry information about new Internet mailing lists. And fourth, information about new mailing lists is often posted on existing mailing lists.

Before diving into uncharted, potentially treacherous waters, I advise both "newbies" and experienced users alike to consider the following advice with respect to mailing lists:

1. "Lurk" (that is, spend some time reading postings on a mailing list for awhile before submitting a post) to get a feel for what types of messages are appropriate, and the "culture" of the list.

2. Read the FAQ (frequently asked questions) file, which is periodically posted as a message on many lists so that the list does not get clogged up with the same queries over and over.

3. Save the subscribing information that is sent to you when you join the list. This will be useful when you need to unsubscribe.

4. Consider unsubscribing from very active lists if you are away from your computer for an extended period of time, such as when you are on vacation, particularly if you do not receive your postings in daily digests. Keep in mind that most Internet Service Providers provide limited mailbox storage space, and you can lose all of your e-mail permanently if your allotment of memory is exceeded.

5. Don't "flame" other members. You may not know when the person flamed will be your next boss. Flaming contests sometimes get out of control, and can be very irritating to others on the list, and usually do nothing to further the purposes of the list, which are to share information and network. Be respectful of the opinions of others. My advice has been when someone flames you, even if their attack was unprovoked, simply ignore him or her.

6. Keep the message on topic. You should think twice before posting a message that you judge not to be of direct interest to the list. If you must post something that is off topic, indicate this in the subject line.

7. Don't post commercial messages or advertisements. Information about a new product or service is usually acceptable (check the FAQ file if you are not sure), but most "selling" on mailing lists is verboten.

8. Don't post anything you would be uncomfortable with seeing on the front page of your daily newspaper. There are cases when such publication has occurred (as we all saw firsthand during the Monica Lewinsky scandal).

9. Contribute to the list; don't just benefit from it. The valuable information you receive from your posted query comes from someone who cares enough to do some work, perhaps even some research, to share information with you. You should feel some responsibility to assist others if you can, provided you have something worthy to offer to them.

10. Don't post to the entire list when a private e-mail message would be more appropriate.

11. Use sarcasm and humor sparingly; they don't translate well in e-mail communication.

12. Don't disparage your organization or its board or staff in your messages; they may well be subscribers to the list, or know someone who is.

13. Don't post copyrighted material in your messages without permission from the creator of the material. This is not simply courtesy; it is a legal issue, as well.

14. Make sure that you post messages to the list rather than to the administrative address and vice versa. The e-mail address to subscribe, unsubscribe, or obtain information about a list is different from the address to which you send messages intended for all members of the list.

15. Your responses to posts should be more than "I agree" or "thank you for responding." Try to make your post add something to the discussion, or don't post it at all.

16. Keep appropriate confidentiality in your posting with respect to your organization, its board, staff, and clients.

Appendix G: Sample Code of Conduct

The following is the Code of Conduct for Talk City, an online community located at: http://www.talkcity.com. Reprinted with permission.

The Talk City chat service is provided by Talk City, Inc. In this document, "we" refers to Talk City, Inc., "user" refers to you, and "Standards" refers to our Talk City Standards.

As a user, you are subject to the terms of the Talk City Standards, and other rules that may be published from time to time by Talk City. You may also want to read our Home Page Standards, Privacy Policy, and Child Safety Information.

Talk City is currently provided as a free service to users who agree to abide by the terms and conditions of our Standards. Talk City reserves the right to change the nature of this relationship at any time. Users who violate the terms of our Standards may be banned permanently from using Talk City.

Talk City is a commercial chat service, and not a public chat network. Your right to speak freely here must be exercised with courtesy and self-restraint. When you enter Talk City, it is the same as entering any real privately owned facility, like a conference room, movie theater, restaurant, or shopping mall. The manners and laws of real life apply, and we have the right to remove you if you exceed the Standards below.

When you enter a chat room in Talk City, it constitutes your acceptance of the terms and conditions listed below. If you do not agree to abide by our Standards, please do not enter Talk City chat rooms.

At Talk City, we wish to promote communication in an atmosphere of mutual respect. We call this a "Clean, Well Lighted Place for Chat." We remind all of our users that you are entirely responsible and liable for all activities conducted through your chat on Talk City. Here are our standards:

We do not tolerate harassment

We welcome people of all ages, races, religions, genders, national origins, sexual orientations and points of view. We do not tolerate expressions of bigotry, hatred, harassment or abuse, nor will we tolerate threats of harm to anyone.

Because we encourage discussion and exchange of ideas, we do not allow threatening, defamatory, abusive, tasteless or indecorous statements. For the same reason, we do not allow sexually explicit material in conversations, room titles, room topics or nicknames.

We recognize that kids and teens need to have rooms that nurture them. Rooms with the designation of "4Kids" have standards that, in addition to all other standards, do not allow sexually suggestive conversations or names. In addition, we do not allow rooms that suggest or encourage interaction between kids and teens and adults for improper or illegal purposes. For the same reason, we do not allow sexually suggestive innuendoes or double entendres. Topics dealing with human sexuality and other similar subjects can be discussed, but in an educationally structured and monitored environment.

We invite people to open public rooms and to apply for permanent rooms. Creators (Operators) of such rooms must follow our City Ordinances in choosing a room name, topic, and content. We reserve the right to limit the number of redundant open rooms, rooms not starting with a letter in the alphabet, rooms with extraneous characters such as !@#$%&, etc. or extremely long room names. Operators may use the / kick command only if a participant violates one of the City Ordinances. Operators should then contact the City Standards Advisor about the kicked offender (/msg CSA Message).

We encourage chat room participants not to give personal identifying information or passwords to anyone in the chat rooms. Users should be aware that, when they disclose personal identifying information such as their actual name, member name, e-mail address, etc., in a chat room, the information may be collected and used by others to send that person unsolicited e-mail from other parties.

We allow only legal activities

Although this seems obvious, we will not allow any illegal activities. Specifically, we won't let you advocate illegal conduct or participate in illegal or fraudulent schemes. You cannot use our chat rooms (channels) to distribute unauthorized copies of copyrighted material, including photos, artwork, text, recordings, designs, or computer programs. In addition, we do not allow the trading or swapping of images that are sexually explicit, obscene or vulgar. Because there can be no way of ensuring compliance with this section, rooms titled for the purpose of exchanging or swapping images are not allowed. Even though it is not exactly illegal, we will not let you impersonate someone else, including one of our trained chat hosts.

Please do not use a deceptive nickname that would lead people to believe you are a member of the City Conference Crew, Forum Volunteers, or Community Standards Advisors (that is, including the letters TCC, CCC or CSA). People depend on our hosts as official representatives, and respect the fact that they have earned their TCCs, CCCs or CSAs through special training.

Stalking of others, in our chat rooms or in another manner, is a serious offense. In many areas, such behavior is considered to be a criminal act. We reserve the right to release information to the proper authorities, because of a violation of our standards, or because of unlawful acts, if the information is subpoenaed, and if we deem it necessary and/or appropriate.

We cannot guarantee the content of comments that you will receive while you are online. Other people's comments may be offensive, harmful or inaccurate.

While Talk City conducts chats on a broad range of topics, the Talk City staff and volunteer hosts do not offer professional advice of any kind.

Hosts speak from their own experience and voice their own opinions when helpful for conducting a conversation. Chat hosts claim no professional or expertise or authority, and Talk City claims no responsibility for their remarks.

We do our best to encourage comfort and discourage disruptive communication.

Talk City does not allow posting or use of computer programs that contain destructive features, such as viruses, worms, Trojan horses, etc. We also do not allow any bots or scripts on the server, whether they are benign or destructive in intent.

We also discourage disruptive conduct: persistent off-topic comments in a topic-oriented conference, statements that incite others to violate the City ordinances, or the physical act of "scrolling"—repeatedly hitting the Return key in a conference—all are considered disruptive.

The use of pop-ups that are excessively long (more than two lines of text), and the use of pop-ups or sound waves in a repetitive manner that disrupts the topic or conversation in a room, are not allowed. Users inviting others to visit Web sites with content that do not comply with Talk City Standards are considered to be in violation of our Standards and subject to action by the CSA and other staff.

We do not allow unauthorized commercial activity.

We encourage communication between our members, but posting or transmitting of unauthorized or unsolicited advertising, promotional materials, or any other forms of solicitation to other users, in Talk City, except in those areas that may be designated for such a purpose, is not allowed.

Your right to privacy is addressed in our Talk City Privacy statement. You can review a copy of this policy by clicking on the phrase "Your Privacy."

We encourage your participation in upholding City Standards

We want your visit here to be enjoyable. If you have questions about City Standards, or need to report a violation, ask a conference host or a Community Standards Advisor to help you (someone with CCC or CSA attached to their nickname). We reserve the right to immediately terminate or suspend access to our chats for conduct that we believe interferes with other peoples' enjoyment. We also reserve the right to amend or change these guidelines at any time and without notice.

Here is some very specific legal language that we are adding so that our lawyers can have a good night's sleep:

Neither Talk City, its partners, advertisers or third party content providers make any warranty with respect to any content, information or services provided through, or in conjunction with, our chats and our site. Talk City, its partners, advertisers or third party content providers are not liable for conduct by any user in chatrooms, auditoriums, private messages, web pages, profiles, or message boards. Talk City, its partners, advertisers, or third party content providers make no guarantee of the accuracy, correctness or completeness of any information on the site, and are not responsible for: (i) any errors of omission arising from the use of such information; (ii) any failures, delays or interruptions in the delivery of any content or service contained within the site; (iii) any libelous or unlawful material contained within user web pages, resumes, profiles or postings. As a user, you agree to indemnify Talk City, its partners, advertisers, or third party content providers against any and all claims and expenses, including attorney's fees, arising from the use of chat rooms and site. This expressly includes: (i) user responsibility for any and all liability arising from the violation or infringement of proprietary rights or copyrights, and (ii) any libelous or unlawful material contained within user chat comments, Web pages, resumes, profiles, or message board postings.

When in doubt about appropriate behavior here, remember that Talk City is an electronic world, but the people here are real.

welcome to www.socialworker.com
Home of
THE NEW SOCIAL WORKER ONLINE

The place for social workers on the Net.
Bookmark this page and visit us often!

Translate **this page** into French, German, Italian, Portuguese, or Spanish with AltaVista's translation service.

Celebrate being a professional social worker with "I am a Social Worker" buttons. (Makes a great graduation gift for your students or classmates!)

See our JOBS PAGE for current social work job listings. Lots of job listings in many locations!

Announcing:

Our new online store. For easier ordering of all our publications and other products, visit our **secure** store.

[Current Issue of THE NEW SOCIAL WORKER | Back Issues | Careers and Jobs | Online Job Center | Social Work Links | Writing for THE NEW SOCIAL WORKER | Subscription Information | Advertising Information | Book: DAYS IN THE LIVES OF SOCIAL WORKERS | Book: THE SOCIAL WORKER'S INTERNET HANDBOOK | Order Form/Online Store | Social Work Careers Chat Room | Message Board | Send a Letter to the Editor]

Interact

Stop by our **Message Board** and join in the discussion of social work careers. Comment on an existing topic, or create your own.

We also have a **Social Work Careers Chat Room**. Allow a few minutes for the chat page to load. Then scroll down to get a "handle" and begin chatting!

You are welcome to visit the chat room at any time. Rich Bott, a regular visitor to this site, will be in the chat room on **Sunday nights from 9:00-10:00 p.m.** to chat with fellow social work students and social workers. Please join him!

At times when a chat is not scheduled, the chat room may be empty. Don't despair! Go to our message board and join in the lively discussion.

Excerpt from The New Social Worker home page at: http://www.socialworker.com. ©2000. Reprinted with permission.

PART 2
Web Site
Reviews

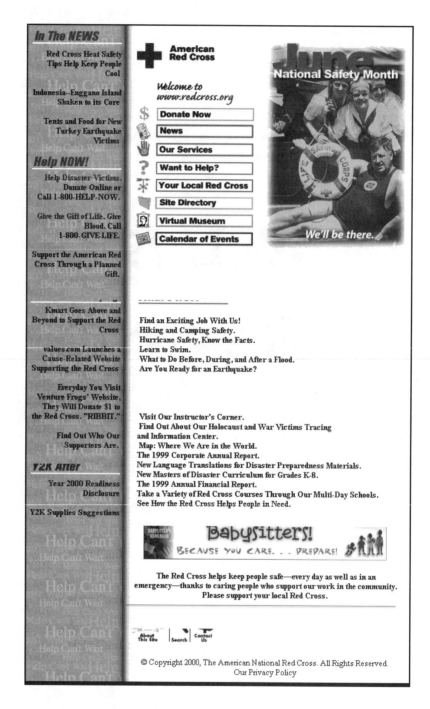

Home page of the American Red Cross. Courtesy of the American Red Cross. All rights reserved in all countries. Visit the American National Red Cross at: www.redcross.org. Reprinted with permission.

Web Site Reviews

Advertising

Internet Advertising Bureau
http://www.iab.net

The IAB is a trade association for those interested in Internet advertising, and there is plenty of content available for public access that serves as a primer for "newbies." You can find meticulously researched articles on the effectiveness of online advertising, standards for banner sizes, case studies of successful Internet advertising campaigns, templates for banners, and information about statistics and trends related to the topic.

Charity E-commerce Site Examples

American Cancer Society
http://www.cancer.org

The content here is first class, but there is not much e-commerce going on at this site. A bookstore (http://www.cancer.org/bookstore) permits books to be ordered online using a secure form, with four major credit cards accepted, and there is participation by the organization in the Amazon.com Associates program.

American Lung Association
http://www.lungusa.org

There is a "store" link on the home page, but it was "under construction" at the time of this review. Knowing that the store will be up soon, however, made me breathe easier. A news banner scrolls across the home page. There are pages for donations of money, for planned giving, and for contributors to donate vehicles. Best of all, there is a plethora of content on this site that isn't provided anywhere else, assuring a steady stream of visitors.

American Red Cross
http://www.redcross.org

This is the site that continues to make headlines by setting online fundraising records. The home page links to for-profit partners that promote contributions to the organization, such as Charity Frogs (see page 18) and Values.com. There are secure forms for giving, and a planned gift page. There are individual pages for the Turkish earthquake disaster and Kosovo Refugee relief with news about what's happening there and a frame to facilitate donations. A page links to the home pages of corporate donors who have contributed at least $250,000 to the ARC. The site has lots of pictures, colorful icons, animations, and is one of the best e-philanthropy sites on the Web.

Girl Scouts of the USA
http://www.gsusa.org

This searchable site required me to use its search engine to find the "store" (http://www.gsusa.org/shop) rather than having a link on the home page. On this page was a link to the Girl Scout Catalog, and a link to a shopping mall that sold Girl Scout related items such as books, camping gear, sports equipment, uniforms, and a gift shop. One useful file accessible from the store was a table of shipping and handling charges with information on rush orders. The site included information about making donations, but did not have an online donation form.

Goodwill Industries
http://www.goodwill.org

From the home page, there is an icon to "Enter the Goodwill Shopping Village" and one as well for Goodwill's auction site, http://www.shopgoodwill.com, developed by a commercial provider, Kruzin Internet Services (http://www.kruzin.net). There was minimal information about cash donations and planned giving to the organization—simply files informing potential contributors that they should contact their local affiliates to make donations. A missed opportunity.

Metropolitan Museum of Art
http://www.metmuseum.org

Everything about this custom-designed site is "state of the art" (see page 24 for a more comprehensive description and history). The non-commercial aspects of this site are integrated tastefully and unobtrusively with the commercial content, which includes a store with a secure shopping cart. Memberships are sold online, and donations are solicited as well.

Copyright

Columbia University's Copyright Resources for Education Online (CREDO)
http://www.ilt.columbia.edu/text_version/projects/copyright/ILTcopy0.html

This page has a primer focusing on the basics of copyright as well as other intellectual property legal issues. Included in these practical and easy-to-digest documents are hyperlinks to the agencies and laws that are described.

Cornell Law School's Legal Information Institute
http://www.law.cornell.edu/topics/copyright.html

This page includes legal citations for copyright laws, court decisions, and international conventions, many in full text, and links to groups, organizations, publications, and government agencies with an interest in copyright developments.

Electronic Frontier Foundation's Intellectual Property Page
http://www.eff.org/pub/Intellectual_property

Documents relating to intellectual property are archived on this site, including a Copyright FAQ written by Terry Carroll in 1994 and periodically posted to newsgroups on the topic (see http://www.eff.org/pub/Intellectual_property/copyright.faq).

U.S. Copyright Office
http://www.lcweb.loc.gov/copyright

This site has all of the documents and forms you need to register your copyrights, and includes links to applicable laws, federal regulations, and treaties. Be sure to read the FAQ document at: http://www.loc.gov/copyright/faq.html.

Domain Name Selection and Registration

The Internet Corporation for Assigned Names and Numbers (ICANN)
http://www.icann.org/

ICANN is responsible for accrediting domain name registrars throughout the world. Here you can find the names of, and links to, all of the organizations that are authorized to register domain names directly (although you can obtain indirect domain name registration services through almost any Web host).

Network Solutions
http://www.networksolutions.com

Included on this site is a dot-com directory (businesses must register to be included in this free listing), a WHOIS lookup service, free and commercial Web site development tools such as a guestbook and profanity filter, Web hosts and ISPs, and, or course, domain name registration services.

Register.com
http://www.register.com

Registering at this site entitles you to a free three-page Web site. An excellent FAQ file provides answers to questions about domain names. See http://www.register.com/faq/getting-started.cgi.

Donor Information

Charities Today
http://www.charitiestoday.com

Founded in 1998, this Internet-based site includes *The Encyclopedia of Charities,* which includes information about charities that have enrolled in the program. The site includes interviews and guest columns relating to philanthropy, and eye-catching charts and graphs of data relating to 501(c)(3)s that is embarrassingly out of date. Click on "Today's News" for summaries of news stories found in the *Chronicle of Philanthropy* within the last two weeks.

The Chronicle of Philanthropy's Careful Donor Page
http://donors.philanthropy.com

This is a spinoff of the *Chronicle of Philanthropy's* conventional online site that is focused on the needs of donors for information about giving. In addition to content from the biweekly newspaper, it has reports on charities compiled by the Philanthropic Advisory Service.

Council of Better Business Bureaus (CBBB)
http://www.bbb.org

Four links on the home page are of interest to charities: (1) Check a National Charity Report. This page has reports on scores of national, regional, and local charities prepared by the Philanthropic Advisory Service of the BBB. These reports are excellent sources of information about each charity listed, and include financial, fundraising, governance, and program information and whether they meet the standards of the CBBB (see below). (2) Order Give But Give Wisely. *Give But Give Wisely* provides a quick reference listing of over 200 of the most-asked-about national charities. In addition to indicating who meets and does not meet the BBB's standards, *Give But Give Wisely* notes which organizations have not provided information despite the BBB's written requests. The free publication is also available online. (3) Ask or Complain about a Charity. This links to a form to complain about a charity, and the complaints are investigated by the Philanthropic Advisory Service. If desired, the complainant's name will not be shared with the charity. (4) Charity Standards Revision. This links to a Discussion Document: *Issues for Consideration in the Revision of the CBBB Standards for Charitable Solicitations.* This document has a link to the current standards.

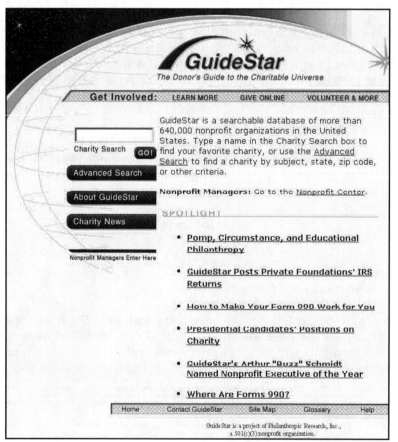

The GuideStar home page at http://www.guidestar.org.
Reprinted with permission.

GuideStar
http://www.guidestar.org

GuideStar is a searchable database of more than 640,000 charities. The search provides a capsule summary of the organization and whether detailed financial reports, information about the mission and programs, the names of its board members, and links to the Web site, or the actual 990 in PDF format are available for viewing. Although the organization does not provide resources for online giving, it provides links to its partners that do.

National Charities Information Bureau
http://www.give.org

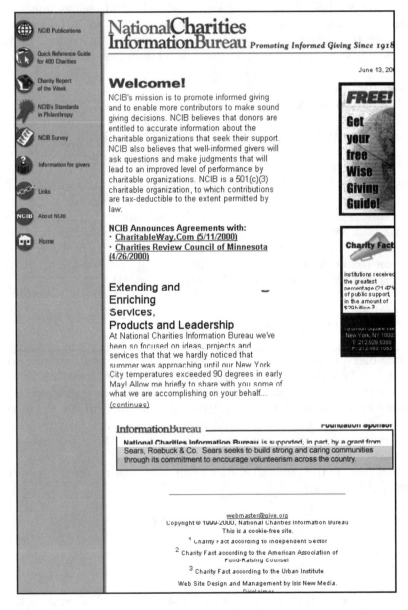

The National Charities Information Bureau at http:// www.give.org. Reprinted with permission.

NCIB is a four-decades-old 501(c)(3) that seeks to provide independent information about charities to aid donors in making their philanthropic decisions, much of which is based on a review of 990s of charities with annual budgets in excess of $500,000. On this site is a quick reference guide to 400 charities, a copy of the NCIB Standards in Philanthropy, and useful online publications for donors. Among them is a *Wise Giving Guide*, a *Tips for Giving* booklet, and an FAQ.

E-Commerce—General Resources

E-Commerce Innovation Center
http://www.cf.ac.uk/uwcc/masts/ecic

This site is based at Cardiff University in Wales, and has an assortment of case studies (all Welsh examples), research, and essays (click on "E-Commerce" on the home page for an introduction to the subject). The links page has some resources that are obscure, but useful, including some e-commerce-related publications that I didn't see on any other pages.

OnlineOrders.net
http://www.onlineorders.net

This is one of the most useful e-commerce sites on the 'Net. Here you can find links to free e-commerce software such as shopping carts and hit counters (and commercial versions as well); find articles about merchant accounts and other e-commerce issues; read about the latest e-commerce news; receive coaching electronically on how to choose and register a domain name; and find publications, software, and other services for the purpose of driving traffic to your Web site. There are hundreds of links to associate programs. The site is searchable, and is the first site to visit if you want to add a store to your existing site. If you don't yet have a site, visit this site second, after Web Monkey (see below).

Webmonkey
http://hotwired.lycos.com/webmonkey/

This site has almost everything you will ever need to build, maintain, and market your Web site, with an online "how-to" library. One useful resource is a 6-chapter tutorial on e-commerce (see: http://hotwired.lycos.com/webmonkey/e-business/building/tutorials/tutorial3.html). Not sure how to integrate animation, video, MP3 files, and graphics on your site? Articles and tutorials walk you through the process. Whether it's learning the basics of HTML or learning about how to handle fonts, creating tables or frames, this is the place to gather basic information on Web site design and more.

Electronic Mailing Lists

About.com Nonprofit Mailing List
http://NONPROFIT.about.com/gi/pages/mmail.htm

Visit the above URL to subscribe to a mailing list with news and views about the nonprofit sector.

Charity Channel
http://charitychannel.com/forums/

You can read descriptions, subscribe, unsubscribe, and view archives of more than 40 free electronic mailing lists of interest to nonprofits. According to the site, more than 30,000 subscribe.

Chronicle of Philanthropy Online
http://philanthropy.com/services/register.htm

Subscribers to this publication receive a biweekly summary of top stories that are appearing in the current issue, and this mailing list usually arrives in your electronic mail box before the "dead tree" version arrives in your U.S. Postal Service mail box. Consider it a valuable "heads up."

E-Philanthropy Hotsheet (Mailing List)
http://www.internet-fundraising.com/hotsheet.html

This list, compiled by Allison Schwein, provides the latest trends in nonprofit technology, and includes directions to find more resources on Web sites.

Egroups
http://www.egroups.com

This is a free service that lets you create a mailing list. Each group receives up to 20 MB of storage space, and all messages are archived. Private chat rooms are available, as well as a polling service.

Microsoft's b-Central Listbot
http://www.Listbot.com

This service provides more control over administration of the list to the list creator rather than the vendor, but requires a $99 fee for Listbot Gold. The Gold version of the software permits you to escape the ubiquitous advertising that you are subjected to when you utilize the free version.

Online Fundraising Mailing List

This moderated list was revived in August 1999 by Michael Gilbert of The Gilbert Center in Seattle, WA. Discussion is lively and topical, and includes the active participation of practitioners, vendors, and consultants. To subscribe, send email to autoshare@gilbert.org with the words "subscribe fundraising" in the body of the message. The idea for this book and many of my columns for *Contributions Magazine* originated from questions and comments I read on this list.

The Philanthropy News Network
http://www.pnnonline.org/pj_alert.cfm

This free mailing list is a service of *The Philanthropy Journal,* and is subscribed to by more than 15,000. While this list includes news of general interest to nonprofits, it is highly salted with technology issues of interest. Many of the advertisements that are included by sponsors highlight vendors that provide e-commerce solutions. It arrives in your mailbox twice weekly, and there are occasional special issues.

Fundraising on the Internet

About.com
http://nonprofit.about.com/careers/nonprofit/msubonl.htm

This page has links to excellent resources on Internet fundraising.

Online Fundraising Resources Center
http://www.fund-online.com/musings/index.html

This collection of essays by Adam Corson-Finnerty and Laura Blanchard is a fascinating and well-written look at e-philanthropy. Many are based on their postings to the Cybergifts electronic mailing list. The site includes teaching materials from classes and presentations, and chapters from the CD companion to their book *Fundraising and Friend-Raising on the Web*.

Silicon Planet
http://www.siliconplanet.com

This site was under construction when reviewed, but advance publicity touted this site as a place to find a free library of current advice and case studies about online fundraising, tools to build Web sites and create online communities, plus information about the firm's fee-based fundraising services.

Fundraising—Online Auctions

CauseLink.com
http://www.causelink.com

This company places a link on participating organizations' Web sites that lets visitors participate in auctions of brand-name goods, such as jewelry, toys, and electronic items. The retailers provide a minimum accepted bid. The nonprofit receives 15% of the winning bid, plus any additional donation the auction participant desires to provide. CauseLink handles all of the transaction tasks, including order fulfillment, and provides customer service. The link to the auction site has the logo of the participating nonprofit and links back to the organization.

CharityCounts.com
http://www.charitycounts.com

Auctions are just one of the services this firm provides to charities. An Auction Tutorial file guides new users through the mechanics of setting up an auction.

Communitybids.com
http://www.communitybids.com

The site provides Web sites to hold charitable auctions, and provides a step-by-step tutorial on how to set up an account and administer the auction. The fees are a flat $10 to create the online auction site, $1 for each item placed for auction, and a sales commission based on the price of the item auctioned that ranges from 1.25% (for items selling for more than $1000) to 5% (for items selling for less than $25). When this site was reviewed, the FAQ was not operational.

eBay
http://www.ebay.com/charity

This site is becoming the auction site of choice for charities that want to harness the track record and experience of one of the largest Internet companies in the world. Click on "How to Info" for information about free registration and how to prepare an "About Me" page that is viewed by prospective bidders. The site conveniently posts testimonials from successful charities, such as HandsNet. Read their stories and get ideas about how to generate more income for your organization than you first envisioned.

FundraisingAuctions.com
http://www.fundraisingauctions.com

Participants fill out an online form entering a description of the item, the amount they want the bidding to start at, and information about how much of the final bid will be donated to charity, if any. The site includes a disclaimer that the service is intended only for nonprofits who are selling items for fundraising purposes, and those who violate this policy will be barred from the system.

Ten97
http://www.ten97.com

Ten97 is a full-service auction turnkey operation for nonprofits, whose services include managing inventory acquisition, collection and distribution of funds, control and fulfillment of auction inventories, production of the auction site including the generation of digital images and descriptions for each item, event marketing, and public relations. The firm has a lot of experience in conducting celebrity auctions.

WebCharity
http://www.webcharity.com

Web Charity was launched in July 1998 to help nonprofits convert in-kind donations into cash. According to the Web site, the firm has raised over $150,000 for charities and has more than 600 nonprofit members. The service charges no fees to participating charities. Unusual for a for-profit company, the firm discloses financial information on its site at: http://www.webcharity.com/wc/results.asp

Fundraising—Click to Give

Charity Frogs
http://www.charityfrogs.com/ and *http://www.venturefrogs.com*

This site pledges to donate money to charity for every time a unique visitor clicks on a button on the site, with one donation permitted per person per day. Participants receive an electronic thank you that has a link to a commercial sponsor/advertiser. The current beneficiary charity when this review was written was the American Red Cross.

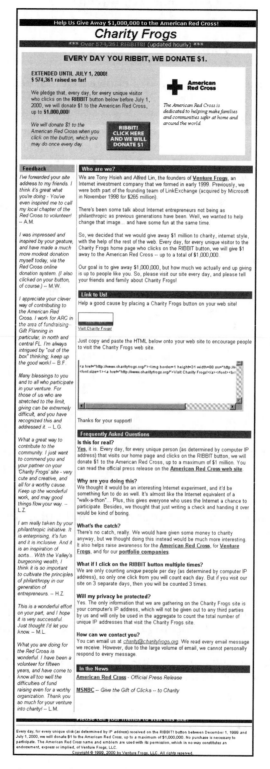

**The Charity Frogs home page at:
http://www.charityfrogs.com.**
Reprinted with permission.

The Hunger Site
http://www.thehungersite.com

 Visit this site and click on the "Donate Free Food" icon that results in the site sponsors making a donation to a food bank. Each sponsor pays one half cent per donation, which buys a quarter cup of food. When I clicked last, there were six sponsors. According to information on the site, more than 200 metric tons of food are donated weekly to the United Nations World Food Programme. Click on the "shopping" icon and you are transported to an online shopping mall where up to 15% of the purchase price is donated to the UN food program.

OnGiving.com
http://www.ongiving.com

This site enables Web users to raise funds for their favorite charity by viewing online advertisements while they are surfing the Web. This is accomplished by signing up for the service and downloading application software and installing it on their computer. The software displays advertisements while the person is online. Eighty-five percent of ad revenue received by OnGiving.com is funneled to the charity, up to 40 hours per month per viewer. The charities can participate by promoting the service and providing a link to it on their Web sites. A demo is provided at the OnGiving.com Web site.

Fundraising—Online Shopping Malls

4Charity.com
http://www.4charity.com

Boasting more than 150 merchants, this site is one of the few that pledge to donate all of their merchant rebates to selected charities. In addition, the chairman and co-founder of the company has pledged to donate all of his stock to charities that participate. Donations are forwarded to each designated charity every month, and the site includes information on how much is donated for purchases from each merchant. Among the 60 charities who are beneficiaries so far are Project Hope, Amnesty International, and the American Red Cross.

Charitycounts.com
http://www.charitycounts.com

The home page of this site has some interesting content for charities. So far, 43 charities have signed up, along with 36 retailers, although the site doesn't make clear how much the participating charity receives from purchases. This site also supports a service that permits donors to send a gift card, by e-mail or snail mail, announcing donations made in the name of a recipient. Click on "Talking Charity" for original content of interest to charities, or "Latest News" for developments in the sector.

Charitymall.com
http://www.charitymall.com

This is one of the few sites that pledge to pass along 100% of the rebates to the designated charity. Commissions provided by the more than 100 merchants range from 1-50% and are posted on the site. The home page describes the "typical" rebate as "3-30%." Registrants must set up a separate e-mail account for transactions with merchants in order for donations to be credited to charities, and the purchasers must have a separate account for each charity they designate for the rebate. Charities can download promotional materials from the site's sponsor.

GreaterGood.com
http://www.greatergood.com

 The approximately 2,000 charities that participate qualify for a custom-designed shopping site that permits the charity to select the merchants included. Charities are guaranteed at least 5% of the purchase price of goods purchased, and this amount can rise to 15% for purchases made with certain retailers. Charities are paid on a quarterly basis. The company also provides its own customer service to supplement that of the more than 80 participating merchants.

iGive.com
http://www.igive.com

iGive.com is the venerable granddaddy of online philanthropic/shopping services, at the ripe old age of two years. As I write this, the service has more than 100,000 members. More than 9,000 causes have received payments from iGive.com, amounting to more than a half-million dollars. Individual payments (which are conveniently posted online) range from a penny to several hundred dollars. Each of the more than 200 merchants who participate negotiates an amount rebated to the charity of between .5% and 15%. All of the rebate is sent to the charity, usually within 60-90 days after the purchase is made. iGive.com receives its own commission from the merchants that is equal to or less than the amount received by the charity. The sponsors will make a $10 donation to your designated charity when you make your first purchase.

ihelpsupport.com
http://www.ihelpsupport.com

The site donates $5 to a designated charity for every member who signs up with the service, and as I write this, most of the 153 charities listed as beneficiaries have been credited with $5. Participating charities are expected to collect e-mail addresses from their supporters, who receive promotional e-mails from the site. According to site sponsors, the average charity earns 50% on sales made, although there is a need for more clarity on what actually is the benefit to the charity. The site also includes a free auction service for charities.

ireachout.com
http://www.ireachout.com

This sponsor provides 2-25% of the purchase price to participating charities, and posts the percentage donation range for each merchant. What makes this site stand out from the rest is that it offers free electronic greeting cards to members with 10 cents donated to a designated charity for each card sent. Although there is a cap on the amount that can be raised in this fashion, depending on the number of members who designate a particular charity, a large charity can theoretically receive as much as $10,000 by launching a card-sending campaign among its members if 5,000 or more sign up for the service. Donations are distributed to charities quarterly.

Shop2Bless
http://www.shop2bless.com

This site is geared to helping Christian ministries, although all charities are eligible. The administrators keep 50% of the commissions from more than 50 merchants, providing from 5-12.5% to the charity. The commission percentages are posted for each merchant. One major drawback for members is that they must provide a confirmation of their purchase to the site in order for their designated ministry/charity to be credited. There is also a $10 minimum before a beneficiary will receive a check.

The igive.com home page at: http://www.igive.com.
Reprinted with permission.

Shop2Give
http://www.shop2give.com

This site permits purchasers to choose from a database of all 640,000 tax-exempt charities in the IRS Master List database as the recipient of donations. Charities can monitor the amount of shopping traffic and their contributions by using a password in a protected area of the site. Ninety stores are participants, and the donation to the designated charity ranges from 1-15% with the site retaining up to 50% of the merchant rebate.

Shop4Change.com
http://www.working4change.com/shop

This is the site established by Working Assets, an organization that has a 15-year history of collaborative agreements between business and charities that have raised more than $20 million. Working Assets provides 5% of purchases made from its more than 90 participating merchants to "progressive" nonprofits that are selected each year by the program's membership. The home page features a participating charity. As I write this, members are voting on how 1999 proceeds are to be divided among 50 established charities, such as Doctors Without Borders, Oxfam America, Human Rights Watch, and the Global Fund for Women, and which charities might be included in the current year's program.

ShopGenerocity.com
http://www.shopgenerocity.com

The administrators of this site retain 50% of the merchant rebates, which range from 1-50%. Participating charities can receive a commission of 10% of what is earned by charities they refer to the site. They are also eligible to receive a share of advertising revenue generated by the site. Charities receive software that permits them to select the merchants they wish to have on their site, and provides promotional materials as well. You can find a search engine on this site that rewards users with a penny donated to their favorite charity for each search requested.

Fundraising—Portals

All Charities
http://www.allcharities.com/home.html

This portal, according to site information, permits you to make a donation to any one of 680,000 charities and have all of your donation go to that charity. All donations are deposited directly into the bank account of the Internet Giving Foundation, which then distributes a monthly check to designated charities. Donors may use this service to donate anonymously to the charity they choose, but still receive receipts and substantiation letters to qualify for their tax deductions.

CharityWave
http://www.charitywave.com/

This is another portal in which charities receive 100% of funds that are donated, with all transaction costs paid for by Wave Systems Corp. Privacy of donations is assured by the site. When reviewed, 46 charities were participating, including some well-known national charities, such as People for the American Way, the Union of Concerned Scientists, and the National Wildlife Federation.

CreateHope.org
http://www.createhope.org

This portal site provides online giving, volunteer opportunities, educational resources about philanthropy, nonprofit sector news and current events, evaluation tools, and more. Donations can be made by secure credit card forms or by calling an 800 number. Donors receive a full tax deduction, and the site management deducts an 8% transaction fee. This is one of the more pleasant-looking Internet home pages. There are hundreds of charities to choose from, but most of the major charities have obviously chosen not to partner. Clicking on the search term "cancer" led to just two small charities with the term in their names, and two more with the term in their organization's description.

Helping.org
http://www.helping.org/

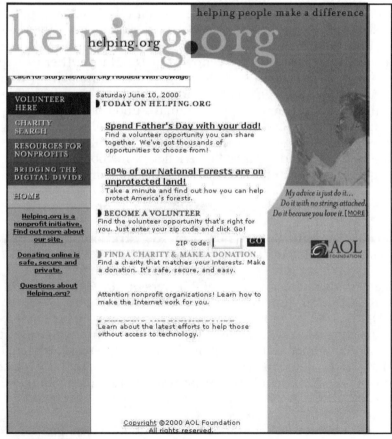

The helping.org home page at: http://www.helping.org. ©2000. Reprinted with permission.

As you might expect from management affiliated with America Online, this site is a beauty to behold. The portal does not take a commission on online donations and the charities pay no fees or costs other than the standard credit card transaction fees. The AOL Foundation pays all other costs. The site maintains donor privacy. Some of the partners who worked with the foundation to create the site are well-known charities and voluntary sector advocates, such as the American Red Cross, the Urban League, the Benton Foundation, and Independent Sector. Click on the "Nonprofit Resources" button accessed from the home page to find tools and publications you can use to build and maintain your Web site, free Internet and e-mail access, and Web site hosts. This site has a volunteer match database where you can use a wizard to type in preferences and the search will find a match. When I typed in my Zip code, it returned 17 volunteer opportunities within six miles. This is a resource that every nonprofit should know about and take advantage of.

Independent Charities of America
http://www.independentcharities.org

These searchable portal sites for charities raise funds for charities relating to animals, children, education, environment, faith-based, health and medical research, human rights, international relief, military/patriotic, and women/family. Each has its own Web site, such as Educate America! (http://www.educateamerica.org), Conservation & Preservation Charities of America (http://www.conservenow.org) Do Unto Others (http://www.duo.org), Children's Charities of America (http://www.childrenscharities.org), Health and Medical Research Charities of America (http://www.hmr.org), and Animal Funds of America (http://www.animalfunds.org). Donations can be made online to any charity via check, credit card, or gift of stock. A 501(c)(3) organization itself, the organization reviews and certifies its beneficiary members annually. Donors can give to member charities online using a secure form.

Fundraising—Internet Regulation

The Internet Nonprofit Center's Uniform Registration Statement Page
http://www.nonprofits.org/library/gov/urs

This page provides access to a printable version (in PDF format) of the Uniform Registration Statement (URS), which is accepted by 38 states and the District of Columbia (six of these require a supplemental form, which is also available at this site). This form is useful to charities that solicit charitable contributions in multiple states. The page also has FAQ files and an HTML file of the URS, which is useful for reading on a computer screen. The FAQ details the registration requirements in all states and DC.

Online Compendium of Federal and State Regulations for U.S. Nonprofit Organizations
http://www.muridae.com/nporegulation/

This site has valuable information about charitable solicitation regulation by each of the states and the District of Columbia. There are lots of links to related sites.

State Regulation of Internet Solicitation

http://www.muridae.com/nporegulation/documents/
internet_solicitation_law.html

This page accesses Paul E. Monaghan, Jr.'s 1996 paper from Yale Law School titled *Charitable Solicitation Over the Internet and State-Law Restrictions*, written under the direction of Professor John Simon. Clear, concise, and provocative.

Fundraising—Service Providers

DonorNet

http://www.donornet.com

DonorNet.com, a Colorado-based startup with a division that caters to the needs of nonprofit charities, offers services similar to those of RemitNet and more. In addition to having the capability to collect and process online donations, the company also offers database administration, pledge and membership enrollment, event registration, ticket sales, auctions, and product sales. For umbrella fundraising organizations such as United Ways, Women's Way, and corporate employee giving programs, the firm offers Give@Work software, a suite of Web-based tools that automates employee pledge submission and campaign management. According to information from the company's Web site, this software can be customized to meet the organization's charitable objectives, provides for various payment options including payroll deduction, and integrates with existing user databases while maintaining the organization's control over donor data to address security and privacy concerns. See: http://donornet.com/giveatwork/index.htm.

e-Contributor

http://www.econtributor.com

This commercial company integrates its engine with the Web site of its clients to provide for secure, online fundraising, payment processing, data collection, and reporting. It also offers volunteer recruitment and member communications services such as targeted text and video e-mail.

Entango

http://www.entango.com

For a 5% transaction fee, this company provides nonprofits with donation processing, unlimited access to online campaign management pages, and unlimited donor access to online donation histories.

GivingCapital

http://www.givingcapital.com

This Philadelphia-based firm provides Web-based fundraising solutions to charities, including creating an online community that is attractive to donors and potential donors.

LocalVoice

http://www.localvoice.com

LocalVoice.com provides Internet-based fundraising software to help nonprofits build state-of-the-art Web sites that attract donors and provide for secure transactions and privacy (see page 103).

Membership4U.com
http://www.membership4u.com/

This company processes nonprofit organization memberships, dues, and donations for a 2.99% commission with free Web-hosting and the use of secure forms to process credit cards.

RemitNet, Inc.
http://www.remit.com

RemitNet offers nonprofits a suite of products, for a fee, which includes online donations, event registration and memberships, and marketing help.

seeUthere.com
http://www.seeuthere.com

seeUthere.com, launched in September 1999, offers special event planning and coordination services to nonprofit organizations and others. By partnering with twenty other companies, the company does everything to make an event successful from sending invitations (through e-mail, fax, or direct mail) to purchasing gifts, providing volunteer sign-ups, and administering online fundraising. Many of the services are free, and the fees for sending invitations, processing online donations, and selling tickets to an event are posted on the site (click on "fees" from the home page).

General Nonprofit Internet Resources

2du.com
http://www.2du.com

This site uses banner ads to list events and business messages in almost 45,000 local communities. Charities partner with the firm by selling advertising for $30 each, and the charity keeps $13.50.

Changing Our World
http://www.changingourworld.com/

This site has excellent current online articles accessed from its home page on e-philanthropy, nonprofit e-commerce, and related issues. Mike Hoffman & Associates, the site's founders, offer iCampaigns®, which works with charities to increase the amount of funds they raise on the World Wide Web. You can receive a free, monthly electronic newsletter by subscribing with a form provided at the site.

The E-Philanthropy Hotsheet (Web Site)
http://www.internet-fundraising.com/np-resources.html

The searchable site, initiated and maintained by Allison Schwein of AMS Consulting, has lots of articles on e-commerce and e-philanthropy, including an excerpt of Chapter 6 of this book. There is a report on charity malls, and plenty of links to articles on these topics.

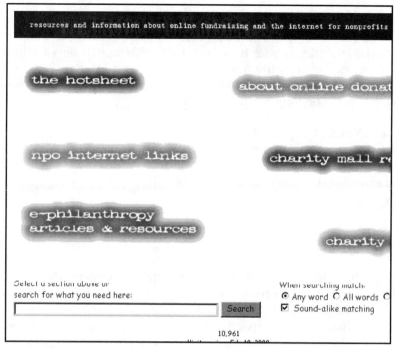

The E-philanthropy Hot Sheet home page at: http://www.internet-fundraising.com/np-resources.htm. Reprinted with permission.

Resources for Fundraising Online
http://www.nonprofits.org/npofaq/misc/990804olfr.html

This is a list of links begun in August 1999, compiled and updated by Putnam Barber, the editor of *The Internet Nonprofit Center.* The best thing about this site is its comprehensiveness, listing nearly two hundred Web sites, and there is an edit log to track changes made to this list. Its main shortcoming is that most of the material about each site comes from the site owners, rather than being independently reviewed. Despite that, this compilation is the first place to go for information about new nonprofit and for-profit Web startups of e-commerce and e-philanthropy services that cater to nonprofit organizations.

Rick Christ's Nonprofit Internet Resources
http://www.rickchrist.com

Edited by Rick Christ, a private nonprofit technology and marketing consultant, this site offers useful information on e-mail for fundraising and marketing. Over 100 articles are archived for searching, including a comprehensive research paper on Internet Fundraising. You can subscribe to two free e-newsletters here.

Money Transactions

Cybercash
http://www.cybercash.com

Visit this site to learn more about one of the companies that pioneered electronic commerce software and services for merchants. Founded in 1994, this company supports over 22,500 e-commerce merchants through its

CashRegister service, processes over 10 million online transactions per month, and has sold over 145,000 copies of its payment software. When I last visited the site, it was hawking a $49.95/month service that appeared to provide everything a nonprofit would need to set up an e-commerce application, including Web hosting and a merchant account—without any setup fee or long-term contract.

Electronic Funds Corporation
http://www.achnetwork.com

This commercial site provides a variety of online electronic funds transfer services.

Ecash.com
http://www.ecash.com

eCash.com has developed innovative electronic payment methods, and has pilot projects with internationally known banks such as Credit Suisse, Deutsche Bank, and the Bank of Austria. More than $32 million in ecash transactions have been recorded in these pilot programs since 1994.

PayByCheck
http://http://www.paybycheck.com/

PaybyCheck is the largest Internet check transaction company, offering online check processing, verification, volume check writing, billing, and address verification. This is a useful e-commerce service to accommodate those who do not have a credit card or who do not want to use a credit card over the Internet.

VeriSign Internet Trust Services
http://www.verisign.com

This firm is the most-recognized and trusted brand name in Web site certification authentication. The company's software supports encryption of customer data, and assures visitors that you are who you say you are, so that they will know that the credit card information they transmit to you over the Internet will be safe and secure. VeriSign's Secure Site Services are backed by the NetSure Protection Plan, an extended warranty program against economic loss resulting from the theft, corruption, impersonation, or loss of use of certificate, underwritten by Lloyd's of London. For a free guide to Internet security, click on *Securing Your Web Site for Business* from the home page, which refers you to an online form rather than the publication itself. The $349 no-frills service includes up to $25,000 of insurance coverage and authority to display the VeriSign Secure Site seal.

Online Communities

DraGoNet
http://www.drexel.edu/ia/DraGoNet.org

This is a good example of a charity (Drexel University of Philadelphia) using an online community to build relationships with potential donors, in this case, alumni. The site is "rented" from the Bernard C. Harris Publishing Company (see: http://www.alumniconnections.com/), which custom-designs online community Web sites for schools and other organizations.

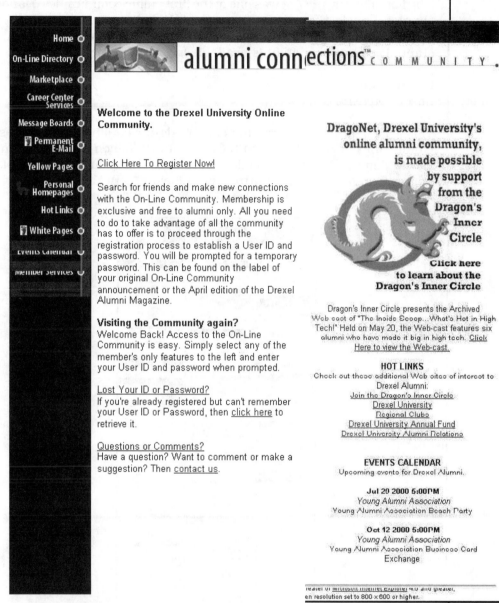

Welcome to the Drexel University Online Community.

Click Here To Register Now!

Search for friends and make new connections with the On-Line Community. Membership is exclusive and free to alumni only. All you need to do to take advantage of all the community has to offer is to proceed through the registration process to establish a User ID and password. You will be prompted for a temporary password. This can be found on the label of your original On-Line Community announcement or the April edition of the Drexel Alumni Magazine.

Visiting the Community again?
Welcome Back! Access to the On-Line Community is easy. Simply select any of the member's only features to the left and enter your User ID and password when prompted.

Lost Your ID or Password?
If you're already registered but can't remember your User ID or Password, then click here to retrieve it.

Questions or Comments?
Have a question? Want to comment or make a suggestion? Then contact us.

DragoNet, Drexel University's online alumni community, is made possible by support from the Dragon's Inner Circle

Click here to learn about the Dragon's Inner Circle

Dragon's Inner Circle presents the Archived Web cast of "The Inside Scoop...What's Hot in High Tech!" Held on May 20, the Web-cast features six alumni who have made it big in high tech. Click Here to view the Web-cast.

HOT LINKS
Check out these additional Web sites of interest to Drexel Alumni:
Join the Dragon's Inner Circle
Drexel University
Regional Clubs
Drexel University Annual Fund
Drexel University Alumni Relations

EVENTS CALENDAR
Upcoming events for Drexel Alumni.

Jul 29 2000 5:00PM
Young Alumni Association
Young Alumni Association Beach Party

Oct 12 2000 5:00PM
Young Alumni Association
Young Alumni Association Business Card Exchange

The Drexel University online community at: http://www.drexel.edu/ia/DragoNet. Reprinted with permission.

HandsNet
http://www.handsNet.org

HandsNet is an online community for public policy advocates and activists. Launched in 1987, it was one of the first online communities. HandsNet charges a modest fee of $99 per year for Webclipper, a personal clipping service and professional library for human services professionals. A substantial amount of content is available free for non-members.

Ibelong, Inc.
http://www.ibelong.com

This is a for-profit company that custom-designs online communities, including the one used by the AFL-CIO for its 13 million members. You can view a demo of the firm's model home page designed to be suitable for nonprofit organizations at: http://netu.ibelong.com.

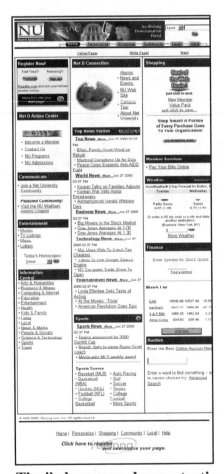

The ibelong.com demonstration nonprofit online community template at: http://netu. ibelong.com. Reprinted with permission.

The New Social Worker
http://www.socialworker.com

This site is a good illustration of an online community that was constructed by an in-house, self-taught person. The owner pays $9.95/month for Web site hosting. It has a lot of free bells and whistles that can be found on sites described in this section of the book, including a "tell a friend" form, chat room, message board, visitor counter, and site statistics generator. It is also the place to purchase many of my other nonprofit management and nonprofit technology books using a secure online form.

Online Community Report
http://www.OnlineCommunityReport.com

The Online Community Report is a free twice-monthly e-mail newsletter about online communities. The current issue and back issues are available at the Web site.

Privacy

David Whalen The Unofficial Cookie FAQ
http://www.cookiecentral.com/faq/

This document could have been called "Everything You Wanted To Know About Cookies But Were Afraid To Ask." It is a soup-to-nuts encyclopedia covering what they are, how they work, why they exist, and how to create them for your Web site. Must reading for anyone interested in the privacy issue (and, if you ever ask me if I am interested, I'll tell you that it's none of your business!).

Privacy Policy Statement Generator
http://www.oecd.org/scripts/PW/PW1.asp

This is a template that can be used to plug in information about your site in order to create a nifty privacy policy statement for posting. It is a project of the Organisation for Economic Cooperation and Development. To find this page, you may need to use the search engine provided, since there is no direct link.

TRUSTe
http://www.truste.org

For a fee, Web sites that meet certain standards can display a logo of this organization, which was established to set up privacy standards and provide sanctions against participants that violate the standards. It has become the Web privacy equivalent of the "Good Housekeeping Seal of Approval " (see page 46).

Publications—Electronic

Chronicle of Philanthropy
http://www.philanthropy.com/

This is the online version of the biweekly tabloid that is must reading for nonprofit organization executives. Some features, such as the searchable database of archived articles, are free for subscribers to the publication. Articles can be read free online, and many developments in e-philanthropy and nonprofit-related e-commerce receive coverage in the general section as well as the Technology column. Clicking on the "Technology" icon links you to four articles in the current issue.

E-Commerce Times
http://www.ecommercetimes.com

Here you can find full-text, current articles about e-commerce topics; e-commerce-related cartoons; business news; links to e-commerce products and services; and much more.

Non-Profit Online News
http://www.gilbert.org/news/

This free online newsletter is available at the Web site, or by a weekly e-mail. It is a publication of the Gilbert Center, founded by Michael Gilbert, a well-known private nonprofit consultant who also established the Online Fundraising mailing list. The lively, chatty news articles in this e-zine are spiced with hyperlinks that often lead to interesting surprises of interest to those who follow nonprofit technology issues.

NonProfit Times (Online)
http://www.nptimes.com/

The online version of *NonProfit Times* includes the fulltext of lead articles from the tabloid, which is published 21 times annually.

Nonprofit Xpress
http://www.npxpress.com

Nonprofit Xpress is an online newspaper that reports on philanthropy and the nonprofit sector. It is published at its Web site every weekday by the A. J. Fletcher Foundation of Raleigh, N.C., and arrives every Friday in the e-mail box of subscribers.

Philanthropy News Network
http://www.pnnonline.org

This site is a spinoff of the *Philanthropy Journal.* a Raleigh, N.C.-based newspaper for the nonprofit sector that discontinued its print publication in March 2000. When I reviewed this site, it was being re-engineered with a launch date scheduled for the fall of 2000. Full-text articles on issues of interest to nonprofits, and generous coverage of technology issues, are available at this site. A free e-mail with capsule summaries of articles in the current issue is available for subscription. The e-mails, which also market PNN-sponsored technology conferences, include advertising from vendors selling e-commerce and e-philanthropy products and services.

Technology Insights
http://www.technology-insights.com

This site has the full text of current and back articles published in this quarterly magazine, which is published both in print and online. The parent firm, Third Sector Technologies, has some valuable content on its own site, which can be found at: http://www.thethirdsector.com.

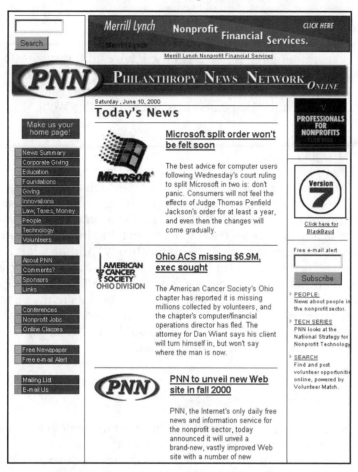

The Philanthropy News Network Online home page at: http://www.pnnonline.org. Reprinted with permission.

W. K. Kellogg Foundation
http://www.wkkf.org/Publications/e-phil.pdf

This file, in PDF format, is a Kellogg report titled e-*Philanthropy, Volunteerism, and Social Changemaking,* published in February 2000.

Publications—Conventional

Contributions Magazine
http://www.contributionsmagazine.com

This is the Web site of a tabloid-sized newspaper that is published six times annually and targets its articles to an audience of nonprofit professionals. Many of the columns are about the new technologies available for nonprofit fundraising and e-commerce. Some of the material in this book first appeared as my column for *Contributions.*

Search Engines

Alta Vista
http://www.altavista.com

AltaVista is a search engine. A search of the term e-philanthropy found 110 matches. I use Alta Vista when I am searching for a specific site and I have a long string to search for (for example, the full title of an article that I suspect may be posted somewhere on the Web).

Ask Jeeves
http://www.askjeeves.com

Ask Jeeves is a search engine that uses common English questions that the user types in rather than the esoteric Boolean search terms required by many of its competitors. It is also a search engine of search engines. Type in a question such as "Where can I find information about e-philanthropy?" or simply type in "e-philanthropy" and its search spider will return some of the most likely matches you are looking for from a handful of popular search engines, such as Web Crawler and Alta Vista. (I'm not sure why, but Ask Jeeves had access to as many as ten of these search engines when I first became enamored with the site in 1999.) Using this site may save time if you would otherwise be performing searches on more than one search engine.

Dogpile
http://www.dogpile.com

Dogpile is a search engine and directory that performs metasearches of other search engines when you activate its "metasearch" function. Type in your keywords, and the engine will find matches in at least 10 other popular search engines. It is a service of Go2Net.com (http://www.go2net.com).

Google
http://www.google.com

Google is one of the newer search engines, launched in late 1999. It tends to be the search engine I use the most after Yahoo!. I searched on the term "e-philanthropy" and found 242 matches.

HotBot
http://www.hotbot.com

HotBot is a search engine and directory. "Submit a Web Site" can be found at the bottom left of the home page. A search on "e-philanthropy" found "more than 10,000" matches.

Infoseek
http://www.infoseek.com

Infoseek is a directory and search engine, and is particularly suitable for performing specialized searches, such as for sounds and graphics. "Add URL" is found at the bottom left of the home page. A search of the term "e-philanthropy" found 67 matches.

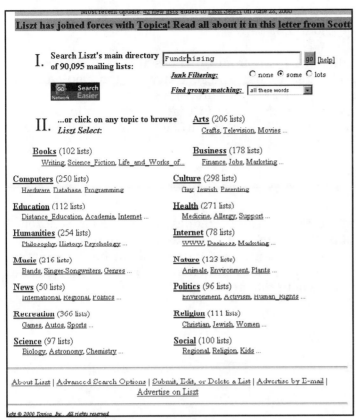

**The Liszt.com home page at: http://
www.Liszt.com.** Reprinted with permission.

Liszt's Directory
http://www.liszt.com/

Liszt's Directory is a leading directory and search engine of mailing lists
and newsgroups.

Lycos
http://www.lycos.com

Lycos is a directory, search engine, and online community. "Add Your
Site to Lycos" can be found at the bottom left of the home page. A search
on the term "e-philanthropy" yielded two hits based on user traffic and
224 Web sites that had the term in a search of the complete Lycos catalog.

Nonprofit Zone
http://www.nonprofitzone.com

There is a lot of content of interest to nonprofits at this site, but what
caught my eye was a free service, among many offered here exclusively to
nonprofits, that will register your nonprofit Web site with 50 of the top
Internet search engines and 50 of the top Internet directories. The staff
will also create metatags based upon the most effective keywords and
send them to you. See: http://www.nonprofitzone.com/free/wwwsp.asp.

Northern Light
http://www.northernlight.com

One aspect that differentiates it from others is that it has access to nearly 7,000 full-text publications. The good news is that you can find many matches for search strings that are unavailable on many of the other search engines. The bad news is that the descriptions of the matches are free, while the full text of the articles is provided for a modest charge.

PhilanthropySearch.com
http://www.philanthropysearch.com

This site is a directory and a search engine specialized for nonprofit-related sites. "Submit Your Site" is located at the bottom right of the home page. A search on "e-philanthropy" found just one hit. This search engine is a relatively new entry (1999) and may yet become an important tool in the arsenal of the nonprofit sector.

WebCrawler
http://www.webcrawler.com

WebCrawler is a search engine and directory. "Add your URL" is located at the bottom left of the home page. A search on e-philanthropy found just one hit.

Yahoo!
http://www.Yahoo.com

Yahoo! (which is an acronym for "You always have other options") is a directory, search engine, and online community. If you only register with one directory, this would be my choice. Yahoo!'s main directory is enormous, and well organized—an important combination for the Internet—resulting in a valuable and easy-to-access way to find what you need. Sites are added to the directory both by the staff of Yahoo!, who proactively look for sites, and by people who want their sites placed in the appropriate categories. Click on "How To Suggest a Web Site" at the bottom left of the home page for directions. You will be asked to suggest an appropriate category for your site. Had there been a category for "e-philanthropy," my search on the term would have taken me to the directory. Instead, it returned 43,451 matches.

Security

Edge.Fireplug.Net
http://edge.fireplug.net

The Edge Firewall is available for free downloading on this site, and can be installed on a 486 computer.

GNU Privacy Guard
http://www.gnupg.org

This is the site where you can download free privacy software and the manual that goes with it.

The Interhack Web—Internet Firewalls
http://www.interhack.net/pubs/fwfaq

This is a comprehensive FAQ file on Internet firewalls prepared by Matt Curtin and Marcus Ranum, computer science researchers, and last updated in November 1999.

Network Associates' Pretty Good Privacy (PGP)
http://www.pgp.com

This commercial site is the vendor of the leading encryption and firewall software.

Tec-Ref.com
http://www.ntresearch.com/firewall.htm

This paper by Tom Sheldon on Internet firewalls is based on his 1996 book and updated in 1998.

Webmonkey Web Development Tools
http://hotwired.lycos.com/webmonkey/backend/security/

Visit this site to access an encryption tutorial, articles on protecting customer data, and privacy-related files.

Taxes

National Governor's Association
http://www.nga.org/106Congress/SalesTax.asp

This page provides a briefing on Internet retail sales taxing issues, including the status of pending Congressional legislation.

Trademarks

U.S. Patent and Trademark Office
http://www.uspto.gov/web/menu/tm.html

This is the official information page for the federal government office that administers trademark law. You can register for a trademark online at this site, check the status of a pending or existing trademark, or find basic information about the process and the law.

Columbia University's Institute for Learning Technologies
http://www.ilt.columbia.edu/text_version/projects/copyright/ILTcopy2.html#3c

This document is part of a larger monograph entitled *Summary of Copyright Basics*, but includes a primer on trademark law, as well.

Web Site Design

Anexa.com
http://www.anexa.com

The headline on the home page of this site boasts that using the software at this site, you can "create your free, personalized online community in one minute." The services include chat rooms, discussion forums, an events calendar, a classified ads page, a member database, a guestbook, and mailing lists, among others.

ArsDigita

http://www.arsdigita.com

You can download free software here that will add to the usefulness of your Web site. One such program, *Vox Populi*, allows you to set up polls on your site with real-time calculations of the results. You can custom-design the content and design of the results pages. *Lusenet* is a newsgroup (discussion forum) software program, and it provides e-mail alerts to subscribers when additions are made to threads. Uptime will monitor your Web server and alert you by e-mail when it is down.

AtomZ.com

http://www.atomz.com

This site offers a free search engine for your Web site, provided that there are no more than 500 pages. You are not required to show any banner advertising, but must display the company logo on searches (the site's FAQ can be found at: http://www.atomz.com/help/faq.tk#20).

Barry's Clip Art Server

http://www.barrysclipart.com/

This is a good site for free, downloadable clip art to spice up your Web pages.

BeSeen

http://www.beseen.com/

Here you can find free chat rooms, guestbooks, hit counters, bulletin boards, and stores. For example, viewers can select from eight styles of free counters, each advertising the BeSeen site. By registering (free), the HTML code for the counter you select is e-mailed to you and you simply paste it into your Web page file.

Bluestreak

http://www.bluestreak.com

If you are looking for custom-made banners or to just get ideas on how banners are designed, this is a site worth visiting. There are plenty of demos of the commercial company's designs. The company performs other Web-based services as well, but based on the quality of its products, this is likely to be a banner year for Bluestreak.

BraveNet Web Services

http://www.bravenet.com/samples/counter.php

By registering (registration is free), viewers can access up to three free hit counters of many styles and colors.

Brian's Guide To Web Page Hit Counters
http://www.zoomnet.net/~skeppler/

When reviewed, this site had ratings (1-5 stars) and information about eleven free hit counters and five commercial counters, including graphics showing what they look like on your page.

CAST Center for Applied Special Technology
http://www.cast.org

CAST is an educational, nonprofit organization that uses technology to expand opportunities for all people, including those with disabilities. The site has tools and links to promote that goal, including "Bobby" (http://www.cast.org/bobby/), a Web-based tool that analyzes Web pages for their accessibility to people with disabilities.

Charity Focus
http://www.charityfocus.com

Launched in April 1999, Charity Focus consists of more than 400 volunteers who build Web sites for nonprofit organizations. Contact this organization for free help in designing, developing, and marketing your nonprofit Web site. A $100 administration charge is levied on nonprofits using the service that have annual budgets in excess of $200,000. More than 250 organizations have taken advantage of these services. An online application form is provided for nonprofits who seek help. Testimonials and examples of sites developed by the organization's volunteers are accessible at the site. An FAQ (http://www.charityfocus.org/faq.html) explains the details.

CNET
http://www.cnet.com

This is clearly one of the most useful sites on the 'Net for finding free software to set up and embellish your Web site. Use the Directory from the home page and click on "Enterprise Business—E-Commerce...," then find "e-commerce downloads" under "More CNET Resources." The automatic search engine found more than 70 matches of freeware, shareware, and free product demos to download, including free shopping carts, Web product catalog software, and inventory control software. There are other pages filled with software, free for downloading, to build your Web site from scratch.

FreeMerchant.com
http://www.freemerchant.com

Over 85,000 businesses are using the free online store builder available at this site, including the publisher of this book. FreeMerchant.com offers a free host for your online store, a secure shopping cart, unlimited space for your online catalog, a Web traffic log, an e-mail account, a calculator for taxes and shipping, a coupon creator, and technical support. Participants must log in with a username and password, but registration is free for all of these services.

Future Focus
http://www.futurefocus.net/web.htm

Future Focus is a commercial firm that has developed Web pages for planned giving. According to the site, the content is provided by a law firm that has specialized in estate planning for over fifty years. The site includes sample pages. They reside on Future Focus's server in a separate folder and are maintained and updated by its staff. The client's logo and design are mirrored. All contact by the viewers will be with the client, and there is no mention of, or link to, Future Focus.

Helping.org Web Tools
http://www.helping.org/nonprofit/tools.adp#webtools

Facilitated by a partnership between AOL and the Benton Foundation, this page is a series of links to Web development tools, conveniently coded according to whether a fee is required for using any of the tools described.

Refer Me
http://deadlock.com/refer/

This page includes free HTML code (simply cut and paste it into your page) that provides a "Do You Like This Site? Tell a Friend" form. The idea is that someone who likes your page will let a friend of theirs know about it by using your form.

TuCows
http://www.tucows.com

TuCows is another portal for obtaining freeware, shareware, and commercial versions of software, including those with e-commerce applications. It boasts of having more than 40,000 software titles available. The site is searchable by type of software you are looking for and the platform used by your computer. My search on the term "e-commerce" yielded eight matches for products ranging in cost from free to $1500.

Web Content Accessibility Guidelines Working Group
http://www.w3.org/WAI/GL/

This page links to documents describing efforts to set standards to make Web pages accessible to the disabled.

Web Page Backward Compatibility Viewer
http://www.delorie.com/web/wpbcv.html

This site allows you to test how various components of your Web page would look using other Web browsers.

Xoom.com
http://www.xoom.com/webspace

This site provides free Web hosting and the tools you need to build a site, such as free Web page design software (Easy Page Builder 2.0), clip art, security tools, and icons.

Zdnet

http://www.zdnet.com

Zdnet is one of a growing number of portals to find free software you can download, including free voice mail, e-mail, and fax service.

Zoomerang

http://www.Zoomerang.com

This site provides free templates and administrative services to create and post online surveys on your Web site. Several of these templates are designed for the specialized needs of nonprofit organizations. The surveys can also be distributed by e-mail.

Web Sites—Hosting

100 Best Free Web Space Providers

http://www.100best-free-web-space.com/index.htm

This site includes information about free Web hosts, listed alphabetically. Included are reviews and an invitation for viewers to contribute to the list with their own reviews. The site also provides Top Ten lists by categories of Overall, For Beginners, For Experienced Users, For Business, By Shortest Domain, By Banner Treatment, By Web Space, and periodically features a Web site.

Northern Lights Internet Solutions' Freenets and Community Networks

http://www.lights.com/freenet

This searchable site lists freenets and other sites that host free Internet services, compiled by Peter Scott of Northern Lights Internet Solutions.

OnlineOrders.Net

http://www.onlineorders.net

Here you can find a listing of Web-hosting companies that support e-commerce sites.

Xoom.com

http://xoom.com/home/

The site provides unlimited online storage, and 24 hour/day access to your files.

Yahoo! Geocities

http://geocities.yahoo.com/home/

With free membership, you can receive a free Web site with up to 15 megabytes of online storage, with tools provided at the site to build your pages.

Web Rings

Web Ring, Inc.

http://www.webring.org

This is a searchable site that has both a directory and search engine to help you find existing Web rings. Searching on the term "e-commerce" turned up 75 rings, including E-Commerce Business Group (ecbg), E-commerce Business Solutions, E-Commerce Ring, 123, tools for E-Commerce and Web Development, and The Online Shopping and E-commerce Webring. The Directory has "Charity" under "Society and Culture."

Web Sites—Writing Issues

Jakob Nielsen's Web Writing Tips
http://www.useit.com/alertbox/9703b.html

This article, from March 1997, provides excellent tips on writing for the Web.

Miscellaneous

Charitygift
http://www.charitygift.com

This innovative business model to encourage charitable donations is a for-profit venture that permits the public to custom-design birthday, wedding, sympathy, Bar Mitzvah, and other types of cards online using templates. The purchaser includes a charitable donation in honor of the recipient, choosing any one of 680,000 charities. The vendor sends the card by snail mail or e-mail, and funnels 100% of the donation to the charity. The fee for the service ranges from $4.95-$6.95 per card, depending on quantity, plus a 3% credit card transaction fee. An acknowledgment is sent to the donor by e-mail immediately.

Conscious Change
http://www.donate.net

Online donations can be funneled to your charity when viewers send e-cards from this site (see: http://www.donate.net/CCN_assets/memberimages/ecardmkt1.htm).

Netcentives, Inc.
http://www.netcentives.com

Netcentives, Inc. provides Clickmiles to those who make donations to selected charities, such as Toys for Tots, Special Olympics, and (the current designated beneficiary), the San Francisco Boys and Girls Clubs. ClickMiles is the firm's Web-based currency that is redeemable for hotel stays, airline flights, and merchandise for those who purchase goods and services through its programs, partnered with some of the best-known companies (see page 19).

KEY WORD INDEX

V

velocity of communication, 20, 21
vendors, 14, 23, 24, 26, 29, 38, 39, 43, 44, 61, 91, 106, 141, 158, 163, 168
virtual domains, 99
virtual organizations, 12, 90
VISA, 37

W

Web browsers (see browsers)
Web design (see design, Web)
Web hosting (20, 22, 24, 27, 33, 68, 77, 80, 86, 99, 108, 111, 114-5, 116, 129, 137, 150, 152, 154, 157, 166, 167
Webmasters, 22, 24, 27, 111, 116, 119
Web rings, 20, 101, 167-8
Windows Notepad, 27, 34, 116
World Wide Web, 16, 17, 20, 23, 29, 33, 37, 51, 95, 96, 106, 108, 110, 111, 114, 118
writing for the Web, 121-3

X

X-Files, 78

Y

Yahoo!, 18, 77, 78, 79, 85, 100, 111, 160, 162, 167

Index of Site Reviews

For Further Reading

There are scores of helpful books on the market for those interested in finding more information about e-commerce strategies. I have compiled a list of some of the more recent publications that are available from online booksellers such as Amazon.com and BarnesandNoble.com, were recently published, are reasonably priced, and, when available, received good reviews from readers. The number in parentheses is the ISBN, which is useful if you wish to order from your local bookstore or find the title quickly using an online bookseller. The date is the month and year of publication.

1 Business, 2 Approaches: How to Succeed in Internet Business by Employing Real-World Strategies
by *Ron E. Gielgun*
Actium Publishing (0965761762)
September 1998

101 Ways to Promote Your Web Site: Filled With Proven Internet Marketing Tips, Tools, Techniques, and Resources to Increase Your Web Site Traffic
by *Susan Sweeney*
Maximum Press (188506845X)
June 2000

Administrator's Guide to E-Commerce: A Hands-On Guide to Setting Up Systems and Websites Using Microsoft Backoffice
by *Louis Columbus*
Howard W. Sams & Co (0790611872)
July 1999

Allaire Spectra E-Business Construction Kit
by *Ben Forta*
Que Corp (0789723654)
May 2000

America Online's Creating Cool™ Web Pages
by *Edward C. Willett*
IDG Books Worldwide (0764532022)
July 1998

Building Interactive Entertainment and E-Commerce Content
by *Peter Krebs, Charlie Kindschi, and Julie Hammerquist*
Microsoft Press (0735606285)
February 2000

The Business of E-Commerce: From Corporate Strategy to Technology (Breakthroughs in Application Development)
by *Paul Richard May*
Cambridge University Press (0521776988)
February 2000

Buying Web Services: The Survival Guide to Outsourcing
by *J. P. Frenza*
John Wiley & Sons (0471312894)
November 1998

Complete Idiot's Guide to E-Commerce
by *Rob Smith, Mark Speaker, Mark Thompson, and Robert S. Smith*
Que (0789721945)
January 2000

Creating Web Pages For Dummies®
by Bud E. Smith, Arthur Bebak, and Kevin Werbach
IDG Books Worldwide (0764505041)
February 1999

Developing e-Commerce Sites: An Integrated Approach
by *Vivek Sharma and Rajiv Sharma*
Addison-Wesley (0201657643)
June 2000

The 'E' Is for Everything: E-commerce, E-business, and E-learning in Higher Education
by *Richard N. Katz (editor)*
Jossey-Bass (0787950106)
March 2000

The E-Auction Insider: How to Get the Most Out of Your Online Auction
by *Dave Taylor and Susan M. Cooney*
Osborne McGraw-Hill (0072125772)
June 2000

The E-business (R)evolution
by *Daniel Amor*
Prentice Hall (013085123X)
September 1999

E-Business: Roadmap for Success
by *Ravi Kalakota, Marcia Robinson and Don Tapscott*
Addison-Wesley (0201604809)
June 1999

E-Business With Net Commerce
by *Samantha Shurety*
Prentice Hall (013083808X)
November 1998

The E-Commerce Book: Building the E-Empire
by *Steffano Korper, Juanita Ellis, and Jerry D. Gibson*
Academic Press (0124211607)
August 1999

E-Commerce Made E-Z Guide
by *Paul Galloway*
Made Ez Products (1563824434)
January 2000

The E-Commerce Question and Answer Book: A Survival Guide for Business Managers
by *Anita Rosen*
AMACOM (0814405258)
December 1999

E-Commerce Revealed
by *Dan Parks Sydow*
MacCentral Press (0966702638)
May 2000

E-Healthcare : Harness the Power of Internet E-Commerce & E-Care
by *Douglas E. Goldstein*
Aspen Publishing (0834213656)
January 2000

E-mail Business Strategies & Dozens of Other Great Ways to Take Advantage of the Internet
by *Phil Gurian*
Grand National Press (0962163945)
April 2000

E-Profit: High-Payoff Strategies for Capturing the E-Commerce Edge
by *Peter S. Cohan*
AMACOM (0814405444)
May 2000

Enterprise E-Commerce
by *Peter Fingar, Harsha Kumar, and Tarun Sharma*
Meghan Kiffer Press (0929652118)
January 2000

The Entrepreneurial Web: First, Think Like an E-Business
by *Peter Small*
Financial Times (027365036X)
June 2000

Fundraising and Friend-Raising on the Web
by *Adam Corson-Finnerty and Laura Blanchard*
American Library Association (083890727X)
May 1998

Fundraising on the Internet: Recruiting and Renewing Donors Online
by *Nick Allen, Mal Marwick, and Michael Stein*
Strathmoor Press 0962489182
March 1997

The Fund Raiser's Guide to the Internet
by *Michael Johnston*
John Wiley & Sons (0471253650)
October 1998

Futurize Your Enterprise: Business Strategy in the Age of the E-customer
by *David Siegel*
John Wiley & Sons (0471357634)
September 1999

Getting Your Business Wired: Using Computer Networking and the Internet to Grow Your Business
by *William E. Kilmer*
AMACOM (0814470076)
April 1999

Net Ready: Strategies for Success in the E-conomy
by *Amir Hartman, John Kador, John G. Sifonis, and John Chambers*
McGraw-Hill (0071352422)
January 2000

The Non-Profit Internet Handbook
by *Gary M. Grobman and Gary B. Grant*
White Hat Communications (0965365360)
March 1998

Scaling the Great Wall of E-Commerce: Strategic Issues and Recommended Actions
Edited by *Diana Lady Dougan and Fan Xing*
Cyber Century Forum (0967505208)
September 1999

Small Business Solutions for E-Commerce
by *Brenda Kienan*
Microsoft Press (0735608466)
February 2000

Smart Things to Know About E-Commerce
by *Mike Cunningham*
Capstone (1841120405)
March 2000

Survival Guide to Web Site Development
by *Mary Haggard*
Microsoft Press (1572318511)
May 1998

Surviving the Digital Jungle: What Every Executive Needs to Know About eCommerce and eBusiness
by *Jack Shaw*
Electronic Commerce Strategies (0966489039)
May 2000

Web Design: The Complete Reference
by *Thomas A. Powell*
Osborne McGraw-Hill (0072122978)
May 2000

Web Design in a Nutshell: A Desktop Quick Reference
by *Jennifer Niederst and Richard Koman*
O'Reilly & Associates (1565925157)
December 1998

Web Engagement: Connecting to Customers in e-Business
by *Bill Zoellick*
Addison-Wesley (020165766X)
May 2000

Webwise: A Simplified Management Guide for the Development of a Successful Web Site
by *Sam Crowe*
Publishers' Group West (155571479X)
January 1999

The Wilder Nonprofit Field Guide to Fundraising on the Internet
by *Gary B. Grant, Gary M. Grobman, and Steve Roller*
Amherst H. Wilder Foundation (0940069180)
June 1999

About the Author

Gary Grobman received his M.P.A. from Harvard University's Kennedy School of Government and his B.S. from Drexel University's College of Science. He is a Ph.D. candidate in Public Administration at The Penn State University.

He currently is the special projects director for White Hat Communications and is the Contributing Editor for *Pennsylvania Nonprofit Report*. Prior to becoming a private consultant to government, nonprofit, and business organizations, he served for 13 years as Executive Director of the Pennsylvania Jewish Coalition, a Harrisburg-based government affairs organization representing 11 Jewish federations and their agencies. He served almost five years in Washington, DC as a senior legislative assistant for two members of Congress, and was a reporter and political humor columnist for the Capitol Hill independent newspaper, *Roll Call*. In 1987, he founded the Non-Profit Advocacy Network (NPAN), which consists of more than 50 statewide associations representing Pennsylvania charities. He is the author of *The Nonprofit Handbook, National Edition; The Pennsylvania Nonprofit Handbook; The Holocaust—A Guide for Pennsylvania Teachers; Improving Quality and Performance in Your Nonprofit Organization*, and the co-author of three books, including *The Non-Profit Internet Handbook*.

He serves as a regular columnist for international, national, and state publications on nonprofit management and technology issues. He and his wife, Linda, a social worker, author, and publisher, are the parents of Adam Gabriel Grobman.

Reader Survey/Order Form

(use additional sheets if necessary)

The Nonprofit Organization's Guide to E-Commerce

Return to:
White Hat Communications
PO Box 5390
Harrisburg, PA 17110-0390
(or fax to: 717-238-2090)

My name and address, telephone number, or e-mail address (please print legibly):

1. I would like to suggest the following corrections:

2. I would like to suggest the following topics or Web sites for inclusion in a future edition:

3. I have the following comments, suggestions or criticisms:

4. I would like to order ___ additional copies @ 19.95 each plus $3.50 shipping for the first book and $1 for each additional book (PA residents add 6% sales tax or include a Pennsylvania Department of Revenue sales tax exemption certificate). Note: Quantity discounts available.

Notes

Notes

Improving Quality and Performance in Your Non-Profit Organization

by Gary M. Grobman

Managing non-profit organizations in the 21st century will be more challenging and sophisticated than ever before. ***Improving Quality and Performance in Your Non-Profit Organization*** provides an introduction to innovative, creative, and effective management techniques developed to totally transform your non-profit organization. Reap the benefits of the quality movement that is revolutionizing commercial and non-profit organizations, and make your own organization more competitive.

Read ***Improving Quality and Performance in Your Non-Profit Organization*** to learn how you can—

- respond to uncertainty and organizational turbulence
- reduce mistakes and infuse your staff with a quality ethic
- rebuild your work processes from the ground up
- find and implement "best practices" of comparable organizations

Improving Quality and Performance in Your Non-Profit Organization
is a comprehensive, introductory guide to change management tools and
strategies, including—

- Total Quality Management (TQM)
- Business Process Reengineering (BPR)
- Benchmarking/Best Practices
- Outcomes-Based Management (OBM)
- Large Group Interventions (LGI)

It also includes easy-to-read and practical applications of chaos theory and organization theory.

$16.95 5.5" x 8.5" 155 pages   Published January 1999
ISBN: 0-9653653-4-4

The Nonprofit Handbook, Second Edition

The Nonprofit Handbook, Second Edition is the most up-to-date and useful publication for those starting a nonprofit or for those already operating one. This 353-page, 30-chapter **Handbook** is based on *The Pennsylvania Non-Profit Handbook,* a book originally published in 1992 with the help of more than two-dozen non-profit executives and attorneys and now in its 5th edition. Each easy-to-read chapter includes a synopsis, useful tips, and resources to obtain more information. Pre-addressed postcards are included to obtain important government forms, instruction booklets, and informational publications. This essential reference tool includes:

- Information about current laws, court decisions, and regulations that apply to nonprofits—two full pages devoted to each state and the District of Columbia
- Practical advice on running a nonprofit, including chapters on grant-writing, communications, fund-raising, quality management, insurance, lobbying, personnel, fiscal management, nonprofit ethics, and 20 other chapters
- Information on applying for federal and state tax-exempt status
- How to write effective grant applications
- How to hire and fire
- Internet resources for nonprofits
- How to develop a strategic plan
- Recent developments affecting nonprofits

We know you will find *The Nonprofit Handbook* to be an essential resource for every nonprofit organization.
ISBN 0-9653653-2-8 8½" x 11" $29.95+S&H
softcover 353 pages plus index

"The Nonprofit Handbook is must reading. While it will have value as a reference tool to be consulted when needed, I highly recommend that you read the book cover-to-cover to familiarize yourself with the panoply of issues that face the modern nonprofit in the United States."

Joe Geiger, Executive Director
Pennsylvania Association of Nonprofit Organizations

Table of Contents

The Non-Profit Internet Handbook

by Gary M. Grobman and Gary B. Grant

The Non-Profit Internet Handbook is the definitive handbook for non-profit organizations that want to get the most out of the Internet. This is a valuable resource for:

- Non-profit organization executive staff
- Non-profit organization board members
- Those who fund non-profit organizations
- Those who contribute time and money to non-profit organizations.

The Non-Profit Internet Handbook includes:

- How to connect to the Internet
- How to do effective fund-raising and advocacy on the Internet
- How to develop your organization's World Wide Web site
- How to find information useful to non-profits on the Internet
- How to locate on-line sources of government, foundation, and private corporation grants.

Plus—
Reviews of more than 250 of the most valuable Internet sites for non-profit organizations! Internet-related cartoons drawn by the internationally-acclaimed cartoonist Randy Glasbergen, creator of *The Better Half.*
The Non-Profit Internet Handbook is an essential reference publication for every non-profit organization.
$29.95 plus shipping.
ISBN 0-9653653-6-0   8½" x 11" softcover
216 pages plus index

"If you want to understand the Internet, with all it has to offer—if you want to know exactly how the Internet can be useful to your non-profit, how it can increase your interaction with your constituency and serve to spread the word about your organization—if you need to learn to search the Web for reliable, up-to-date information on what is happening in the non-profit world, and the world in general— The Non-Profit Internet Handbook is the perfect gateway to the Internet galaxy."

Sara E. Meléndez, President
Independent Sector

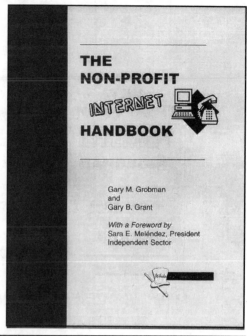

THE
NON-PROFIT
INTERNET
HANDBOOK

Gary M. Grobman
and
Gary B. Grant

With a Foreword by
Sara E. Meléndez, President
Independent Sector

Also Published by
White Hat Communications

Books

Days in the Lives of Social Workers: 50 Professionals Tell "Real Life" Stories
from Social Work Practice
(Second Edition)
Edited by Linda May Grobman

The Pennsylvania Nonprofit Handbook
(Fifth Edition)
by Gary M. Grobman

Guide to Selecting and Applying to Master of Social Work Programs
(Fourth Edition)
by Jesús Reyes

The Social Worker's Internet Handbook
by Gary B. Grant and Linda May Grobman

Why is My Baby Crying?
The 7-Minute Program for Soothing the Fussy Baby
by Bruce Taubman, M.D.

Welcome to Methadonia: A Social Worker's Candid Account of Life in a
Methadone Clinic
by Rachel Greene Baldino

Magazine

The New Social Worker—
The Magazine for Social Work Students and Recent Graduates

ORDER FORM

Telephone orders
(Mastercard or Visa):
717-238-3787
Fax orders: 717-238-2090
Online orders:
http://www.socialworker.com

Visit our Web site:
http://www.socialworker.com

PLEASE SHIP MY ORDER TO:

NAME _____

ADDRESS _____

ADDRESS _____

CITY/STATE/ZIP _____

TELEPHONE NUMBER _____

❑   Enclosed is a check for $_____ made payable to "White Hat Communications."

❑   Please charge my: ❑   MasterCard   ❑   VISA

Card # _____

Expiration Date _____

Name as it appears on card _____

Signature _____

Billing address for credit card (if different from above) _____

Billing City/State/Zip _____

Please send the following publications:

QUANTITY	TITLE		AMOUNT
_____	THE NONPROFIT ORGANIZATION'S GUIDE TO E-COMMERCE	$19.95	_____
_____	THE NON-PROFIT INTERNET HANDBOOK	$29.95	_____
_____	THE NON-PROFIT HANDBOOK, SECOND EDITION	$29.95	_____
_____	IMPROVING QUALITY AND PERFORMANCE IN YOUR NON-PROFIT ORGANIZATION	$16.95	_____

SHIPPING $ _____
SUBTOTAL $ _____
PA SALES TAX (6%) $ _____
(Pennsylvania orders only)

TOTAL DUE $ _____

Shipping charges: $3.50 first book/$1.00 each additional book in U.S. *Please contact us for rates on rush orders, other methods of shipping, or shipping outside the U.S.*

PA Sales tax: 6% tax on books ordered from Pennsylvania, unless accompanied by sales tax exemption certificate

Federal EIN: 25-1719745